SEEING
BEYOND
20/20

By
Dr. Robert-Michael Kaplan, O.D., M.Ed.

I

Published by Beyond Words Publishing, Inc.
Pumpkin Ridge Rd.
Route 3, Box 492-B, Hillsboro, OR 97123
503-647-5109
800-284-9673

The information contained in this book is intended to
be educational and not for diagnosis, prescription, or
treatment of eye conditions or disease or any health
disorder whatsoever. This information should not replace
competent optometric or medical care. The content of
the book is intended to be used as an adjunct to a
rational and responsible vision care program prescribed
by an eye doctor. The author and publisher are in no
way liable for any use or misuse of the material. The
case studies in this book are real; however, the names
have been changed.

Printed by Arcata Graphics, Kingsport, TN
in the United States of America

First printing November, 1987
Second printing June, 1988
Third printing July, 1990

ISBN: 0-941831-01-9

Library of Congress Catalog Card Number: 87-072305

Jacket and book design by Wes Walt
on a Macintosh II with PageMaker,
typeset on a LaserWriter Plus

Cover photograph is a portion of the Supernova remnant in Vela-shock
wave of an exploded star, photographed by David Malin, copyright ©1980,
Royal Observatory, Edinburgh, Scotland (used with permission)

Posters of the Supernova are available from
Hansen Planetarium Publications
1098 South 2nd West, Salt Lake City, UT 84101
800-321-2369

This book is dedicated
to those
who dare to risk
what they feel and see

III

ACKNOWLEDGMENTS

To those who allowed me to see (in chronological order):

My parents Mark and Hilly Kaplan, brother Desmond, sister Barbara, Cecil Clement, D. K. Turnbull, Philip Kruger, Jurie Groenewald, Andre Roos, Mervyn Strauss, Ian Lane, David Varney, A. M. Skeffington, Estelle Herman, Cecil Beinart, Gerry Getman, Stanley Meyers, Jack Liberman, J. C. Tumblin, Kenneth Cooper, Don Pitts, Steve Cool, Ron Harwerth, Ray Gottlieb, Bernard Jensen, my daughter Julia Kaplan, Tole Greenstein, Bob Sanet, Israel Greenwald, Elliot Forest, Marty Birnbaum, Baxter Swarthout, Robert Pante, Werner Erhard, Jack Roggenkamp, Michelle Gold, Dana Sweet, Ian Garbutt, Robert Ficker, Robert Laskowski, Ron Smotherman, Herman and Cornelia Aihara, Herb Dreyer, Robert Pepper, John Downing, Gary Koyen, James Newton, Bev Foster, Michael Grinder, Nancy Hathaway, SEVA, Jean Wright, Louise Hay, Janet Goodrich, Gary Clyman, Lisa Cogen, all my optometric and other students, colleagues, patients, friends, functionally oriented optometrists of the College of Optometrists in Vision Development, pioneering ophthalmologist William Bates, Oregon State Board Of Optometry, and Dean Chester Pheiffer, Dean Willard Bleything and Pacific University for encouraging me to risk and clinically validate the concepts of *Seeing Beyond 20/20*.

Also a special thank-you to my publisher, Richard Cohn, designer Wes Wait, and editor Sara Steinberg.

IV

C O N T E N T S

HOW TO USE THIS BOOK

Seeing Beyond 20/20: Improving The Quality Of Your Vision And Your Life is divided into four distinct parts.

Part One deals with fitness of the eye, specifically at a physical level. First, you will begin to assess the components of your vision fitness. We will take a look at environmental and other aspects of our culture that play a role in the loss of vision fitness. You will learn how your eyes—aided by special vision fitness lenses—can provide feedback to alert you to aspects of your lifestyle that may be affecting your seeing. Finally, we will introduce you to exercises designed to enhance the performance of the individual structures of your eyes.

Part Two explores the idea that fluctuations in vision fitness occur as a normal variation of your daily living. You will begin to recognize how your predominant visual style—being/seeing or doing/looking—affects the way you approach situations in your daily life. We will discuss the behaviors associated with each visual style, and how you can modify your behavior to fit changing life situations.

The way you feed and exercise your body can also affect the way you see. By monitoring the effects of particular foods and levels of physical activity on your vision, you can learn to nurture your body for maximum general and vision fitness.

Part Three introduces the mind's eye. How you interpret events internally can actually have a bearing on your vision. Via clinical cases, you'll see how early events in a person's life later affect his seeing. Discover how high-level vision fitness depends on your right eye and left eye participating harmoniously in what is called "whole-brain" processing.

Part Four gives you an opportunity to begin your *Seeing Beyond 20/20* program for improving your vision in 21 days. A step-by-step, three-week program is described for you to follow.

Each part of this book is self-contained, and I invite you to explore the depth and level of vision fitness that suits your needs.

Parts One through **Three** will introduce you to the theory, research, and clinical evidence underlying the vision fitness approach of *Seeing Beyond 20/20*. I would recommend that you read all three parts at least once through to familiarize yourself with their language and concepts. Use any of the ideas or exercises (vision games) that relate to your particular situation.

Part Four presents a deeper explanation on how to develop a vision fitness program for yourself. Here you'll find a 21-day program that goes into more detail on how to use the different components for improving vision. The material is presented in such a way that, depending on your needs, you might use any or all of the parts of the 21-day program. At certain times you may desire to apply nutritional aspects to your life, while later, wearing an eye patch may look like fun. You could select certain vision games, aerobic or movement exercises, etc., or you might commit to the whole program. Whatever your level of involvement, progress will be made. At any time in the future you can repeat or return to any of the processes.

I often remind my patients and myself that *Seeing Beyond 20/20* is a journey. Sometimes, you may need a rest stop. At other times you will wish to move full steam ahead. Whatever path you follow, perform with great attention to quality!

INTRODUCTION

In our Western culture, having 20/20 vision signifies an ideal level of normalcy. Whether this finding comes from the school nurse, industrial nurse, your eye doctor, or your family physician,when you hear 20/20, you breathe a sigh of relief. If you wear eyeglasses or contacts, they artificially induce 20/20—and you're thankful for that.

But why in our culture is a natural state of clear vision the exception rather than the rule? Why is it that over 80 million of you are nearsighted, and at least six out of 10 of you are relying on artificial devices to see?

Even in the face of 20/20 vision, and regardless of whether or not you wear corrective devices, you may be among the growing number of people who are experiencing increasing degrees of eyestrain. Such symptoms as burning sensations, itching, blurriness, tearing, and aches associated with the eyes usually coincide with a drop in visual efficiency. These behaviors reflect a diminishing ability of the brain to integrate what each eye perceives.

Seeing Beyond 20/20 provides new ways to enhance your vision performance while working with your eye doctor. This approach incorporates techniques developed by the science of eye refraction, diagnosis, and treatment of eye diseases; the technology of contact lenses; and use of medications and surgical breakthroughs.

The new direction outlined in this book is based on one key premise: Just as you can develop your body fitness, you can also improve the fitness of your eyes—how they work together, their health, and their control by the brain. This book presents an opportunity for you to look beyond what you accept as normal; to open up to the reality that, as with your body, improving the fitness of your eyes is now possible.

You may be wondering if I am suggesting that you throw away your eyeglasses or contacts. On the contrary, I suggest that your eye devices, like weights, running shoes, or a tennis racquet, can be utilized as therapeutic tools. In improving vision fitness, you'll use your contacts and eyeglasses therapeutically. This will help your eyes and your brain relearn how to work as a team.

As your vision fitness increases, you will continue to develop a new, therapeutic relationship with your corrective eye devices. If you don't use eye devices, you'll become aware of an increased ability to use your eyes for tasks like reading, fine detail work, computer use, judging distances, enjoying sports, and so on.

By better understanding how your eyes work and can develop or lose vision fitness, you'll become an active participant in their care. Just as your car lets you know when you need to add gas or change the oil, you'll become aware when your eyes are calling for a rest break or a vision fitness exercise.

Seeing Beyond 20/20, then, looks to the future of vision care, which will involve you as an active participant in the prevention of eye problems and the maintaining of high-level vision fitness. This doesn't mean that your eye doctor will become obsolete. Rather, the role of your optometrist or ophthalmologist will be one of teacher, facilitator, or guide in your quest for optimum vision fitness.

As is already the case in China, vision fitness programs can be incorporated into schools, so that children are trained to protect and strengthen their sight through the use of special exercises. Specialized applications of vision fitness are even now being used to help persons with learning and reading difficulties. Persons labeled dyslexic, who face reading challenges such as letter and word reversals, transpositions, and substitutions, are using vision fitness techniques to reduce dyslexic behaviors.

By using the vision fitness approach, you will be improving the quality of your work life. In fact, vision fitness techniques are now becoming part of employee wellness programs in industry and business.

Another benefit of practicing vision fitness is that by gaining insights into the workings of your eyes and the process of vision, you will be better able to understand other points of view. How you perceive a person with whom you are communicating can affect your understanding of what they are saying.

Perhaps you're wondering why this thinking is not commonplace. Why has your past vision care not included prevention and improvement? Why is this form of vision care not readily available?

There are many answers to these questions. I shall attempt to give you a succinct overview by describing my own perspective. In my experience as a professor in two professional schools of optometry in Texas and Oregon, I observed the training of doctors of optometry. The primary approach they were taught for dealing with vision problems involved the application of eyeglasses or contacts. This traditional viewpoint holds that when your eyeball is defective, you need a "corrective" device to compensate for the imperfection. One would think that "corrective" tools like lenses would eventually be removed once the therapy is complete. On the contrary, lens prescriptions typically become stronger! This leads to a greater and greater dependency, as insidious in its own way as a dependency upon drugs, sugar, or alcohol.

I was a victim of that thinking while being trained as an eye doctor. I really believed that by recommending full-strength lens prescriptions for my patients, I could help their eyes to "get better." After working with thousands of patients as an optometrist in Africa and the United States, one day I realized that I was actually contributing to their loss of vision fitness. Having experienced double vision most of my life, and being unable to read for more than 20 minutes at a time, I resolved to discover ways of teaching myself and others to improve vision fitness.

For clues as to where to begin, I had only to look to the progression of my own vision problems. I had always seen 20/20 during childhood. As a young boy in Africa, I recall seeing 25 miles to the coast while standing at the summit of a 7,000-foot mountain. I did, however, have a frustrating problem—I could read words, but could make little sense out of the printed page. For some unknown reason, the messages that my eyes were transmitting to my brain were being scrambled. To my despair and sadness, I was functionally a non-reader! Only years later did I suspect that my reading problem might be related to vision. This suspicion was at least partially responsible for my decision to enter the field of optometry.

The suspicion that I had a vision problem gave way to certainty during my first year of optometry studies in 1968. Studying how each eye sends images to the brain, I one day realized that I was seeing two professors, when actually there was only one. To my astonishment, I became aware that I had double vision more than 50 percent of the time! Did everyone see like that, I thought? Later on I found otherwise.

When I graduated as an optometrist in 1971, I still had double vision about 40 percent of the time. I also had a clue as to the cause: My studies on the relationship between the brain and the eyes had led me to realize that the brain is really in control of the eyes!

Thus I resolved, at the start of my career, to design a program that would train the brain to send more efficient messages to the eyes, and conversely, retrain the eyes to coordinate with the brain. This program would need to serve both patients with 20/20 vision who, nonetheless, had vision deficiencies, and patients who needed corrective lenses to achieve 20/20 vision.

From my clinical studies beginning in 1972, I predicted that 70 percent of people in the first group, who already could see 20/20, had difficulties with coordination of their eyes. I had a sense that 1) these patients could be properly educated to approach seeing as an experience beyond 20/20 vision, and 2) that not being able to read for extended periods, falling asleep while reading, and poor comprehension over time were related to this breakdown in two-eyed coordination. From my clinical experience over the past 15 years, I would state that the 70 percent prediction is 10 percent too low!

My patients who needed corrective lenses provided me with an even more obvious challenge. Whenever I would prescribe eyeglasses for these patients, to my puzzlement and sadness, they would keep returning to receive stronger ones. I wondered why. If the body can repair a wound on the skin, then why couldn't the eyes be trained to restore their natural way of seeing? I began to explore any avenues that looked promising. My own double vision continued to hinder my reading and studying.

In 1973, I left Africa to undertake advanced clinical training at the University of Houston. There I discovered that when patients were taught to relax, their eyesight significantly improved. I also came across the fact that left and right eye movements were somehow related to hemispheric accessing in the brain. In other words, looking to the right implied a left-brain mode of perceiving, and looking to the left allowed one to image and visualize. This stimulated a major theme of my later research: What, I wondered, was the relationship between two-eyed coordination, the two hemispheres of the brain, and vision fitness?

My own experiences also continued to uncover pieces of the vision fitness puzzle. For example, I noticed that consumption of certain foods affected my peripheral (side) vision. When I abused my digestive system with what I called "culprit foods"—which in my case included dairy products, fried foods, and too many eggs—my peripheral vision of details became unstable. It felt like the world was crowding in on me. Since my double vision increased at these times, I ascertained that fitness in my peripheral vision could help keep me from seeing double.

As I became aware of the process of vision, I noticed that my 20/20 eyesight also fluctuated, particularly in my right eye. I usually see better than 20/20—most times my vision is 20/10. Some days I noticed my right eye seeing only 20/20. My double vision was slowly becoming less and I noticed my reading becoming easier. However, I was still wearing special prism eyeglasses to eliminate the double vision. I was determined to achieve single vision without eyeglasses.

After implementing Dr. Kenneth Cooper's aerobic concepts, I had more control of my fluctuating vision. Then I decided to become a lacto-ovo vegetarian, meaning I ate no meat, but still included dairy foods in my diet. These changes allowed me to become even less dependent upon prism eyeglasses. The aerobic exercise, combined with vision fitness exercises, further reduced my double vision.

When I entered the field of education and psychology during 1975, I uncovered the fascinating work of Wilhelm Reich, Alexander Lowen and Charles Kelly. They had found out, it seemed, that the eyes reflect the person within and his or her associated perceptions of the world. For example, nearsightedness seemed related to introversion and fear; farsighted individuals tended to be extroverted, and when undergoing counseling, often dealt with buried anger.

In a natural progression, this brought my attention to the still unorthodox field of iridology, which examines the iris as a means to help ascertain the state of a body's wellness or sickness. Later, study of Chinese medicine strengthened my interest in the eye-brain connection. This system postulates a relationship between the left eye and receptive vision; the right eye is supposedly connected to the expressive vision usually associated in Western culture with masculinity. This raised the possibility that each eye has its own mode of perception. If that is the case, what would happen if the two eyes did not work harmoniously together?

These and many other paths of inquiry seemed to be converging on a major area of investigation—the strong relationship between the mind's eye and the physical eyes. I also concluded that developing vision and recovering eyesight required a multidisciplinary approach. So during 1976-78, I collaborated with professionals in the fields of psychology, education, speech pathology, audiology, medicine, and social work.

From our joint investigation, it became very apparent that the times patients first needed eyeglasses were strongly related to upsetting events that had occurred in their lives. I hypothesized that people actively create or choose to see their world in particular ways. This occurs first at the level of the mind's eye, and later filters down to be measured as distortions in the physical eye. Traditionally, eyeglasses, contact lenses, surgery, and medications were recommended as preferred choices of treatment.

Nineteen seventy-eight was a milestone in my work. I realized that doctors all over the world were using alternative therapies for improving vision, such as vision training, colored light therapy, Bates eye training, trampolines, red/green glasses, prism devices, nutrition, and relaxation. Yet newly trained eye doctors, and therefore their patients, were led to believe that there was no value in these approaches because of the scarcity of scientific studies proving their efficacy.

The writings of John Ott, in particular, revolutionized my thinking about the capacity of the eyes, brain, and mind to restore supposedly lost ability to see when making use of full-spectrum lighting. Light is the basic life force for seeing, so it made sense that such a basic ingredient as light should affect vision. But I had to experiment and demonstrate this for myself by using light and color.

My research on children with reading difficulties demonstrated that reduced peripheral (side) vision could be expanded when specific frequencies of color were focused through the eyes. Most of the children read more effectively and their classroom and home behavior was more manageable.

I also conducted a study investigating the value of using colored light in the treatment of headaches. The successful results convinced me of the value of color and that the process of vision included a neuropsychological dimension.

Let me add that, as usual, I conducted my own personal experiments as well. I recognized my dependency on sunglasses and worked to reduce it. I found that particular colors seemed to have different effects on my body. During this time I was exercising regularly, had become a total vegetarian, was seeing double vision less than 15 percent of the time—and felt wonderful, indeed.

By 1981 I felt I had confirmed that the mind-body-spirit connection was a total reality. Still, one ingredient was missing from the process—namely, the relationship between psycho-emotional events and vision. I began studying with psychotherapists, endeavoring to tap into the reasons why patients make statements like: "I am certified blind without my eyeglasses!" or "My parents wore glasses so I should have them too."

By 1982, after 12 years of developing and testing the *Seeing Beyond 20/20* concepts on over 1,000 people (as well as myself), I was ready to scientifically validate my unique approach. The results of that research are presented in the Appendix.

From 1983 until 1987, I continued to develop *Seeing Beyond 20/20*. I incorporated process-oriented approaches such as working on a large trampoline, using individual and group support, and teaching parents and children together.

Today the vision fitness approach is: teaching parents how to prevent children from developing eye problems, assisting the elderly with debilitating eye diseases, increasing vision performance in dyslexics, teaching eyeglass users how to reduce their dependency on their eyeglasses, helping professional athletes to perform visually at a higher level, and enabling computer users to minimize eyestrain. It is most gratifying to know that some of my patients are flying jets without eyeglasses, and others who used to need eyeglasses to drive cars and buses now have driver's licenses with no restrictions. There are also former dyslexics who are now reading and elderly patients who have avoided costly eye surgery because they used these self-help approaches.

This book is my way of acknowledging the thousands of patients, friends, colleagues, and teachers who assisted me in recovering my vision fitness and in developing *Seeing Beyond 20/20*. The work has been very fulfilling for me, and I feel it is part of a very delicate mission that has just begun.

Improved vision fitness is now a realistic, attainable goal. I invite you to use this book as a resource as you set up a vision fitness program tailored to meet your own goals. If possible, enlist the aid of an eye doctor in your community (see Resources) who incorporates this kind of thinking into his or her practice. Many times such practitioners refer to themselves as vision therapy doctors. Better still, work with a doctor whom you can educate. In turn he or she will educate others. Most important, conduct your own personal vision experiment. You'll see!

PART ONE

FITNESS
OF
THE PHYSICAL
EYE

1. WHAT IS VISION FITNESS?

For their size, your eyes have a greater blood and nerve supply than most other organ systems in the body. It is not surprising, then, that there is a uniquely strong relationship between the brain and the fitness of the eyes.

In the book *Total Fitness*, authors Morehouse and Gross refer to fitness as the ability to meet the demands of one's environment.

Vision fitness refers to your clarity of seeing, the degree of partnership of your two eyes, and making sense of what you see in your environment. We can speak of natural vision fitness (no corrective devices), as well as the degree of vision fitness induced by eyeglasses or contact lenses.

Let's look at the components of vision fitness a little closer!

Clarity of Seeing

Some of you may have observed or have been told that your seeing or vision was not 20/20. This loss of seeing or blurred vision can be considered as a drop in vision fitness.

Even if you naturally have 20/20 vision, you might experience eyestrain, burning or itching eyes, double vision, fatigue, loss of comprehension, or poor attention span. These symptoms or behaviors are also indicative of poor visual fitness or stamina. (In some cases, disease of the eyes produces a loss of natural vision fitness. This disease aspect will be discussed in a later chapter.)

If you have lost your ability to see clearly at the reading distance, this is yet another loss of vision fitness. In this case the focusing/lens system of your eyes is losing its natural ability or fitness to perform. While most eye doctors view this loss as a consequence of natural aging, I have had the opportunity to see patients who prolong their ability to focus clearly and avoid the total loss of focusing by improving their vision fitness.

Mary at age 55 was farsighted (could see far away but less clearly up close) and was wearing recently prescribed bifocals (these provide one focus for near and one for far distances). After one month of using the vision fitness techniques outlined in this book, Mary was able to wear single-vision reading glasses equivalent in power to when she was in her early forties. It's not that Mary was throwing away her eyeglasses. What she did was restore 13 years of vision fitness. She could then see with youthful eyes of about 42 instead of eyes of 55.

You can also use the vision fitness approach if you're nearsighted and/or have astigmatism. Nearsightedness means that you can see more clearly at near than at far distances. Astigmatism usually refers to a cornea that has unequal curvature in the different meridians. This means that you have to focus different amounts and your vision can be affected by blur, straining, and even headaches.

Linda had nearsightedness and astigmatism for over 25 years. Her driver's license mandated her wearing corrective lenses for her entire driving career. Linda began improving her vision fitness at age 36. Within six months of applying the concepts and techniques from *Seeing Beyond 20/20*, she was able to pass the driver's eye test. This meant that after 19 years of driving, Linda was able for the first time to legally drive without corrective lenses, relying solely on her natural vision fitness. At the age of 36, Linda was able to see again as she had when she was age 17. In her case, she was able to accomplish this without any eyeglasses or contacts.

Degree of Partnership of Your Eyes

For those of you who need to wear eyeglasses or contacts, 95 percent of the time eye doctors prescribe a full-strength prescription for 20/20. But in my research on stress and two-eyedness, I have found that in 75 percent of cases, full-strength lens prescriptions for nearsightedness and astigmatism produce distress (unmanageable stress) related to how patients use their two eyes together.

Even more fascinating, there is an 85 percent likelihood that one's doctor will come up with a lens prescription by testing each eye separately. It is assumed that this "single-eye tested" prescription will serve you in a *"two-eyed looking"* world. However, my clinical research has demonstrated that the single-eye tested prescriptions tend to be too strong. I hypothesize that this ultimately plays a role in the lowering of vision fitness.

From my years of clinical testing of both eyes open, I have discovered the need for subtle variations in lens prescriptions, usually a lessening in power. The reduction produces enhanced vision fitness. This is reflected in the way your two eyes will work better together, minimizing fatigue and other eyestrain behaviors. You might question your eye doctor on whether he or she is willing to test your eyes while both are open.

Now, what of the degree of eye partnership in persons who do not wear corrective lenses? A large percentage of you who see 20/20 have difficulty with tasks involving close work. Consider that your eyes are biologically unsuited for the kinds of close work you demand of them. Your eyes are designed for three-dimensional, fast-moving, and multi-focused viewing. However, computer screens, books, newspapers, writing pads, and other fine detailed objects are two-dimensionally focused at one distance. For this reason reading for long periods, looking at a computer screen or terminal, sewing, and fine detailed close work can produce varying intensities of eyestrain. Since these behaviors are unrelated to clarity, I find the difficulty, in 70 percent of cases, to be in how the two eyes work together as a team. Fortunately, vision fitness exercises can assist you in developing greater two-eyed fitness.

Making Sense of What You See

This is the third component of vision fitness. Many of you can hit a fast-moving ball, read words and sentences, and observe data on a terminal screen. However, when you have to process information at higher degrees of understanding, you tend to make less sense of what is seen. For example, you may have 20/20 vision, but find that after reading for a while, your mind wanders, you get sleepy, you daydream, or become bored. Others can enter data into a computer, but find that following logical patterns of thought, retrieving sequenced data consistently, or tracking fast-moving objects for long periods of time becomes fatiguing.

Interestingly, most of you who fall into this third vision fitness category will tend to be a little farsighted. It's as if your eyes are designed for far looking. On the other hand, those of you who wear glasses and contacts for nearsightedness tend to be good readers, excellent students, and have eyes well adapted for reading. Think of it this way: If you are farsighted, your vision fitness will probably be more appropriate for far looking, and with nearsightedness, your vision fitness will be more efficient for near viewing.

All three of the components of vision fitness described above drop off over time. It's as if your eyes run out of gas. Even so, vision fitness, like your body's fitness, can be improved. Your eye muscles can be exercised. The nerve connection from the brain to your eyes can be stimulated. Your body's blood flow to your eyes can be increased. The vision fitness exercises in this book will give you this opportunity. The overall result will be a feeling of well-being.

What Is Your Vision Fitness?

From case histories and clinical research we find that certain behaviors are related to one's level of vision fitness. The following questionnaire* will assist you in knowing which particular behaviors apply to your vision fitness.

Indicate how bothersome these behaviors are, according to your impression, by recording a number between 0 and 10 (0 meaning no problem whatsoever, 10 meaning yes—an unbearable situation).

* Some questions were modified from *Eye Power*, Alfred A. Knopf, Inc. Copyright © 1979, Ann and Townsend Hoopes.

	No	Yes/unbearable

1. Do you have difficulty in completing a close-work assignment (e.g., reading, writing a letter or studying)?
0 1 2 3 4 5 6 7 8 9 10

2. Do you experience difficulty when shifting from one activity to another (e.g., working on a project then going to cook)?
0 1 2 3 4 5 6 7 8 9 10

3. Do you find playing and enjoying tennis, basketball, or any other game involving fast-moving balls and players difficult?
0 1 2 3 4 5 6 7 8 9 10

4. Is your reading speed slow (200 words per minute or less) or have you noticed a drop in your reading speed?
0 1 2 3 4 5 6 7 8 9 10

5. Do you have difficulty reading maps or visualizing geometry?
0 1 2 3 4 5 6 7 8 9 10

6. Do you have difficulty visualizing something you're reading about, or imagining "as if" situations (e.g., on a rainy day trying to imagine the sun shining)?
0 1 2 3 4 5 6 7 8 9 10

7. Have you experienced difficulty with hidden word games, losing sense of direction, or keeping your place while following directions or reading?
0 1 2 3 4 5 6 7 8 9 10

8. Is it hard for you to read for pleasure?
0 1 2 3 4 5 6 7 8 9 10

9. Do you have difficulty concentrating on concurrent events (e.g., following a lecture while taking notes)?
0 1 2 3 4 5 6 7 8 9 10

10. Does your stomach bother you if you read in the back seat of a car?
0 1 2 3 4 5 6 7 8 9 10

11. Is it a challenge for you to organize your visual and mental capacities to read and write effectively (e.g., following an author's point of view or writing a short story)?
0 1 2 3 4 5 6 7 8 9 10

12. Are you disappointed by your performance in reading and writing (see #11, above)?
0 1 2 3 4 5 6 7 8 9 10

13. Is it hard for you to accurately recall or reproduce a drawn, written, or visual presentation of what you've seen? (e.g., observing a scene and then listing what you saw without rechecking)?
0 1 2 3 4 5 6 7 8 9 10

	No	Yes/unbearable

14. Is it also hard to apply the same capacities to solving practical or theoretical problems without use of paper and pen/pencil?

0 1 2 3 4 5 6 7 8 9 10

15. Is your visual attention poorer when there is movement; or when you walk does the horizon appear to move up and down?

0 1 2 3 4 5 6 7 8 9 10

16. Do you find it awkward to judge where objects are (e.g., judging distances when you reach out to find something)?

0 1 2 3 4 5 6 7 8 9 10

17. Do you often misjudge an object's true position (see #16, above)?

0 1 2 3 4 5 6 7 8 9 10

18. Are you bothered by crowds in theaters, department stores, or shopping centers?

0 1 2 3 4 5 6 7 8 9 10

19. Do you have difficulty tracking (following) an object moving laterally or vertically?

0 1 2 3 4 5 6 7 8 9 10

For questions on which you scored five or above, consider that these behaviors relate to your level of vision fitness. By improving your vision fitness, you will reduce your difficulty with those particular behaviors.

You should now be better prepared to participate as an intelligent consumer in your vision care program. Armed with questions and this new insight into your own vision fitness, you can be ready to request the kind of vision care you desire. Find a vision fitness-oriented optometrist or ophthalmologist who will work with you.

2. CAN YOU LOSE VISION FITNESS ?

As outlined in the last chapter, vision fitness covers your clarity of seeing, the degree of partnership of your two eyes, and your ability to make sense of what you see. I also mentioned that loss of visual function due to disease can produce vision fitness changes.

Probably 10 percent or less of the population are born with blurred vision, upset binocularity (two-eyedness), and diseased eyes. But by young adulthood, a disturbing 60 percent of the remaining 90 percent have nearsightedness, farsightedness, astigmatism, crossed or wall eyes, and ocular disease conditions. This provocative statistic clearly demonstrates how we as a culture are slowly losing our natural vision fitness.

This means that from the time we are born until adulthood, our interaction with our environment leads to a drop in vision fitness. From clinical interviews with thousands of patients, I have found the following to be some of the environmental and other factors (not ranked in any order) that play a part in the evolution and development of eye and vision problems:

Inappropriate eating patterns (excessive intake of simple carbohydrates and over-refined foods)

Going to school

Poor reading habits

Air, water, and food pollutants (chemicals, preservatives, etc.)

Excessive sugar consumption

Too little exposure to sunlight

Poorly designed workplaces (includes desks, fluorescent lighting, and chairs)

Achievement-oriented schooling

Lack of physical exercise

Breakup of the traditional family model

Divorce

Frequent moves

Excessive viewing of television

Poorly monitored use of computers

While living in Africa for the first 25 years of my life, I had the opportunity to watch the native African in his natural environment. His eyes move around. They skip focus from close to distant objects. His eyes scan left to right, up and down, and diagonally, stretching the muscles. Your eyes, like the jungle dweller's, are designed to move, stretch, and focus at far distances. You can think of your eyes as biologically still designed for hunting, gathering berries, growing crops, and farming.

However, Westernized culture has developed technology so fast that your natural vision fitness has to be modified: It must adjust to your sitting at a desk, looking at a terminal screen, typing, reviewing computer printout sheets, reading books, working with fine eye-hand coordination, and the myriad of academic and job-related tasks you demand of your eyes. You also expect your eyes to accommodate to artificial fluorescent lighting, blown-in filtered air conditioning and heating, and the bombardment of particles from synthetic carpeting, desks, chairs, paper, inks, and paints. This is a far cry from the green forests, lushly carpeted grasslands, and pristine mountaintops of your counterparts in Africa.

Moreover, you also encounter the challenges of work quotas, deadlines, dealing with co-workers, and financial budgeting. All these stressors can ultimately affect the fitness of your eyes. You may notice that on the days when you are more relaxed, your ability to efficiently use your eyes is greater.

These changes haven't happened overnight. There has been an insidious slow movement to the point where over 70 million persons in the U.S. now require eyeglasses or contacts for nearsightedness. Think of your brain and eyes having to adjust from far looking, like the native African, to concentrating more on school work and office tasks. Nearsightedness is a perfect adaptation. You maintain high vision fitness up close, but less so at intermediate or far distances.

In the last chapter I mentioned the distress that can be brought about by looking through full-strength eyeglass or contact lens prescriptions. Since many of you have been told to wear your prescription full-time, does the distress increase when you look at closer distances? The strength of the distance viewing prescription may be too strong for close work. Seventy percent of the time, your wearing a lens prescription designed for looking at a far distance produces distress while looking at a closer distance. It's not so much that you'll see blurry up close, but you'll experience discomfort, a feeling of tiredness, or even sleepiness while reading, doing computer work, or other close-distance looking. This can also occur for those of you who have 20/20 vision without lenses.

What may be happening is that your eyes are giving you feedback that there's a drop in vision fitness. Over time, your two eyes may no longer be able to cooperate as partners. Your brain, in desperation, may finally decide to shut off one of the images.

Typically, if you receive this kind of feedback, you'll think that there's something "wrong." You may rationalize that you're tired. Others of you may feel your eyes are getting weak or that you need a stronger lens prescription. *Seeing Beyond 20/20* presents another choice. You can view this symptom as you would that red warning light in your car, and take preventive steps to restore your vision fitness.

What are you going to do if you receive feedback that your vision fitness is dropping off? One of the first signs of distress in the body is holding one's breath or shallow breathing. The eyes are situated far away from the heart and lungs, so that shallow breathing can deprive the eyes of essential nutrients. Your vision may appear blurry or grey. Also, more than likely you'll be staring, maybe even with your head thrust a little forward. The best example of this is to watch the people next to you at the stoplight at 5 o'clock on a weekday. Are they staring aimlessly into space, holding their breath and not blinking?

So the first step is to check your breathing. Is it shallow? Breathe differently. Hear the sounds, feel your chest and stomach moving. Blink your eyelids. Check your body posture. It's like pulling up to the service station and checking the water level, the tire pressure, the oil level, and pumping gasoline for your car.

Perhaps you're wondering why you weren't aware of these common-sense ideas. The knowledge of how to improve vision fitness has been available for many years. Being educated in vision fitness is now necessary and important because of the increasing numbers of you who are entering the high technology office and workplace, completing college courses, and becoming involved in hobbies that require exact and precise visual decisions. In the past, you assumed your eyes would stay fit. Now your visual system is no longer able to cope with the environmental demands.

You can ignore the reality of vision fitness loss, and become solely reliant on artificial devices. Alternatively, just as you may be cultivating your body fitness and nutritional well-being, you can begin improving and maintaining your vision fitness. Begin protecting your vision by being aware of when your vision fitness lessens.

3. THE EYES AS A BIOFEEDBACK MECHANISM

Your eyes are the point of focus during most forms of communication. Can you imagine looking at someone's foot while talking to them? Your eyes are indeed the "window to your soul." They reveal an extraordinary degree of non-verbal communication.

In the same vein, if you are aware of your eyes, you will begin experiencing how they provide feedback about the effect of many variables in your life. You may recall from the previous chapter that many factors in your internal (mental and emotional) and external environment can lead to a drop in vision fitness. Looked at another way, the food you eat, the way you exercise, how you relate with others, and satisfaction or upsets in relationships can all give feedback about your seeing.

Clinically speaking, I have observed this vision fitness loss develop over time. It's not like one day you are suddenly nearsighted, farsighted, or have astigmatism. An astute developmentally interested eye doctor can monitor the stages of vision fitness loss. In the same way, as you redevelop fitness in your seeing, so the changes can be measured physically in the eye.

Let's go a little deeper into this concept of how your eyes can act as a biofeedback mechanism. First, a review of what 20/20 eyesight means. 20/20 refers to the measurement of how well you see. When a letter of a certain size can be seen at 20 feet, your doctor will give you a rating of 20/20. On the other hand, if you can see the letter designed for 40 feet at 20 feet, then your rating is 20/40, and so on.

The chart below will assist you in converting this standard eyesight measurement scale into a vision fitness percentage.

VISION FITNESS CHART

Eyesight/Acuity Vision Fitness Percentage

Eyesight/Acuity	Vision Fitness Percentage
20/20	100.0%
20/25	95.6
20/30	91.4
20/40	83.6
20/50	76.5
20/60	69.9
20/70	63.8
20/80	58.5
20/100	48.9
20/120	40.9
20/160	28.6
20/200	20.0
20/300	8.2
20/400	3.3
20/500	1.1
20/600	.06
20/800	.01

As they were trained to do, most eye doctors will determine the refraction (measurement of the eye prescription) needed to provide you with 100 percent ability to perform visual discrimination at 20 feet. Many years ago this standard was set. If you couldn't see 20/20, then it was assumed that you were visually inefficient.

This standard course of treatment, however, is far from an ideal solution: Years ago many of my patients began asking me if there was any way they could improve their eyesight. They were concerned that each time they visited me, I would pass on the news that their prescription was stronger. Chances are you have had that experience yourself, or have heard your friends talking about it.

In response, I began experimenting by reducing the power of patients' lens prescriptions. After a number of research trials, the optimum vision fitness level seemed to be around 83.6 percent. If the level was less than 83.6 percent, the world appeared too blurry and patients' frustration level was too high, thus defeating their natural seeing capabilities. If greater than 83.6 percent, there was not enough blur. This meant that I would measure the patient for 20/40. If they were nearsighted and/or had astigmatism, I reduced the power equally for the two conditions. For farsightedness, I used the far and/or near Eye-C charts (see Chapter 12) and made similar reductions in power.

The overall response from the hundreds of patients who took part in this ongoing experiment was that they loved their new vision fitness prescriptions. Their looking appeared softer and generally produced a calming effect. Everything didn't appear crystal clear. When these patients looked at far distances, closer objects automatically became clearer. This meant that while looking at 10 feet, the vision fitness was back up to 100 percent. In many states, one can legally drive seeing 20/40 at 20 feet.

You might be asking the question, why wear or use a lens prescription that effectively reduces your vision fitness? Besides the behavioral advantages already mentioned, you can begin to teach your brain and your eyes to work more harmoniously as partners.

Let's look at this a little more closely. You have been prescribed a pair of vision fitness lenses designed to give you 20/40 at 20 feet. Your vision fitness percentage would be 83.6 percent. This means that by applying some vision fitness exercises into your daily routine, you can train your brain, eyes, and muscles to make up the 16.4 percent difference. After a period of time you will be seeing 20/20 through this same vision fitness prescription!

This lens prescription can be called a vision fitness type because while wearing the prescription (preferably in eyeglasses because of ease of removal), there will be times during the day when you will be able to monitor changes in vision fitness. As we will see in later chapters, my patients have reported their vision fitness being affected by many elements of their lifestyles, including foods they eat, posture, aerobic exercise, level of stress on the job, strained reading patterns, working for extended periods at a computer terminal, weather changes, and emotional fluctuations. (Just how some of these factors affect vision fitness is discussed in Chapters 6 through 9.)

The advantage of these variations is that you can do something when you receive the feedback. For example, if you notice that your vision fitness drops as job stress increases, you can learn to always take action to alleviate stress. Recall that by breathing deeply you can send extra oxygen and nutrients to the eyes to increase their function. Focusing to your nose (like crossing your eyes) and then looking off into the distance can also bring about a remarkable increase in vision fitness. Over time, by employing vision fitness exercises and making lifestyle changes as needed, you can enable your vision fitness to stabilize at 100 percent through the vision fitness lenses. Then you can have your doctor order an even more reduced lens prescription, and you can begin the process once again.

As you reduce the power in your lenses, your natural vision fitness without lenses will also improve. So overall, you will be wearing lenses that are weaker, you will see more clearly without lenses, and you will be in control of how you use your glasses as opposed to them controlling you.

My clinical experiments on the effects of lens prescriptions produced some very interesting results. When persons looked through lenses that produced 100 percent vision fitness (20/20 vision) versus lenses that gave 83.6 percent vision fitness, less tolerance for handling visual stress was measured. This meant that natural depth perception was reduced, and the full-strength lenses produced strain and fatigue after long-term use.

Thus it seems that the brain "prefers" the 83.6 percent vision fitness prescription. The brain and the eyes then have a chance to be exercised, just like the other muscles of the body that respond well to being exercised. Imagine trying to exercise an injured arm while wearing a tight splint. Loosen the splint and there's more flexibility. The vision fitness lens prescription is like a loosened splint. Looking through these fitness lenses will provide you with a more balanced view.

Vision fitness can be defined a little differently for persons who already have 20/20 vision—and therefore 100 percent vision fitness for looking at details at 20 feet. If you fall into this category, you too can use the feedback principle discussed earlier. For example, recall how you feel after reading for extended periods. Does your comprehension drop off? Does your mind wander or do you become sleepy? Even though you may have 20/20 and high vision fitness for seeing details, your vision fitness for memory retention and recall of many details may be lower than someone who has 20/50 vision, for example. This is a clinical phenomenon that functionally oriented optometrists have noted over the years.

What this means is that the function of your eye muscles and the accuracy of input to the brain from the two eyes needs to be enhanced. Very often persons with natural 20/20 have an impaired ability to coordinate the two eyes together. You would experience this as fatigue after lots of close work, eyestrain or intermittent blurring while working at a computer screen, burning eyes after reading, or dry eyes while concentrating at any other near-point task.

For some of you, a specially designed near-point lens will facilitate greater vision fitness. This will not necessarily provide increased clarity but, rather, a marked change in visual comfort. These lenses have been referred to as "stress relieving lenses" and are also called "focusing lenses." I do strongly recommend that the lenses be used in conjunction with vision fitness exercises, so that you don't become addicted to the lenses. A good check is to see if near-point material seems more blurry when you remove the lenses. If so, the lenses may even be reducing your natural vision fitness.

The purpose for wearing any of these lenses we've described above, then, is to help you see more clearly in the interim while you use special techniques to develop vision fitness. Eyeglasses and contact lenses can now be thought of as therapeutic devices to get you to heightened levels of vision fitness.

In order to have you see with 83.6 percent vision fitness (20/40), your doctor can rewrite your prescription to make it weaker. The amount of reduction is usually on the order of 25 percent. However, the prescription cannot arbitrarily be reduced. Your doctor should examine your eyes and complete a refraction, preferably with both eyes open during the testing. The nearsightedness or farsightedness are reduced in amounts equal to any astigmatism.

Some case examples will further illustrate how reduced power lenses combined with use of the biofeedback principle can help you improve your vision fitness.

Steven, age 24, begins wearing reduced power vision fitness lenses. The following day he goes with his friend George to play a game of racquetball. On entering the court, Steven casually glances around through his new 20/40 eyeglasses and notices that he can just barely make out the time on the wall clock. After 40 minutes of racquetball, as they are leaving the court, Steven once again glances up at the clock. Now the time is perfectly clear (100 percent vision fitness)—his vision fitness has gone up! Steven thus gets feedback that aerobic exercise such as racquetball produces increased seeing.

Of course this calls for a celebration, so Steven and George go off and have a few beers and hearty helpings of nachos, followed by a sugary dessert. As Steven looks around the restaurant, he notices his vision fitness dropping. He is able to see less and less, and he estimates that his vision fitness has dropped down to 73 percent. Again, Steven receives feedback—that certain foods are undesirable.

The choice Steven can then make is to avoid these particular foods, or to exercise more vigorously after consuming these foods.

Another example:

> Anne, age 30, is a data entry computer programmer. Anne spends four to eight hours per day in front of the computer terminal. As an experiment she placed an eye chart on the wall behind her computer terminal. The chart was about 10 feet away, which meant that if she could see the 20 line, then she had 20/40. Each morning Anne checked her natural vision fitness, monitoring the changes. Anne noticed that her vision fitness dropped off after about three hours of continuous work at the terminal.
>
> After consulting with me Anne began a couple of vision fitness techniques, like focusing to the chart and stretching the eyes up and down while paying attention to her breathing (for descriptions of these exercises, see Chapter 12). Breathing for Anne was one of the most important exercises, because whenever the task at the computer became complex, she literally held her breath. Anne also reported staring at the screen without blinking after a few hours of work. By employing the vision fitness exercises, Anne was able to improve her vision fitness to the point where the distressful symptoms were minimal. When she did receive feedback of distress, she employed the techniques to once again increase the fitness. Vision fitness is like body fitness—once you begin you build in a maintenance program.

Patients who have 20/20 or 100 percent vision fitness have also reported fluctuations in their clear seeing when engaged in reading, sewing, crocheting, computer programming, painting, and other near-point activities. This demonstrates that our visual feedback model works even in the case of high levels of vision fitness.

The vision fitness lens allows you to get feedback about any aspects of your lifestyle or environment that affect your physical seeing. The same feedback cannot be obtained as vividly when you are seeing 20/20; this would be like trying to notice if your temperature were fluctuating at 99.0 degrees F when the normal is 98.4 degrees. Your perceptions are not yet adequately trained to perceive those subtle temperature changes. Yet some psychologists and physicians are now training their patients via biofeedback to monitor slight elevations and drops in blood pressure. Why not monitor vision fitness changes through the daily events in your life?

Whenever you notice your seeing becoming blurry, strained, or distorted, take time out from the activity to breathe deeply, focus your attention and your eyes to a different distance, stretch your body muscles, yawn, and blink the eyes. These are easy basic techniques for maintaining high levels of vision fitness.

By the way, as we will discuss in later chapters, your emotional and mental states of mind can affect your vision fitness. It seems that I notice adults—young and old—laughing less than they used to. What do you think will happen to your seeing if you walk around sad or despondent? Smiling, laughing, and being joyous will allow you to increase your vision fitness.

Wear your vision fitness lenses, focus more gently, and smile—your whole body and state of being will feel more relaxed.

PART TWO

NURTURING YOUR EYES

4. EXERCISING THE MUSCLES OF THE EYES

The vision fitness approach calls for an appreciation of the eye parts and how the structures work. Patients stricken with cancer have been taught how to visualize cancer cells being munched away by imaginary friendly cells with mouths. These patients have been able to control, and in some cases eliminate, cancerous tissue. Likewise, vision therapy optometrists and natural vision teachers have taught their patients to see and feel the parts of the eyes and the corresponding control centers in the brain. This visualizing leads to a reduction of eye and mind strain.

Accordingly, this chapter will take you on a journey through the different structures of the eyes, explaining their purpose, how they work, and what strategies can be incorporated to enhance their vision fitness. By learning to picture the anatomy of the eyes, you will also be better able to derive the most benefits from practicing the vision fitness exercises in this and other chapters.

The Cornea

This is the shiny curved part of the outside of the eye. The cornea covers the iris (the pigmented part). The cornea controls 80 percent of the refracting power of the eye.

This structure derives its nutrients from, and is lubricated by, the tears. Tear fluid is distributed over the cornea via blinking. The types of activities you subject your eyes to will determine how much you blink. Looking at a computer screen, reading, watching TV, doing fine detailed work, and driving a car can lead to staring. Typically, blinking stops when you stare. Through video recording, I have been able to demonstrate that the wearing of contact lenses can interfere with the optimum blink rate of every three seconds. What happens for many of you, I suspect, is that the lids treat the contact lens as a foreign body. Your brain sends a message to the lids to blink less. With a lowered level of blinking, you might experience such indications as burning, itching, gritty, heavy, and watery eyes. This is feedback—a reminder to blink. Blinking every three seconds is one of the first ways to enhance your vision fitness.

As I suggest to my patients, catch yourself staring during the day and introduce a blink on the average of every three seconds. Feel the tears (I call them juices) flowing over the magnificent cornea. Thank the different eye structures for the wonderful work they do.

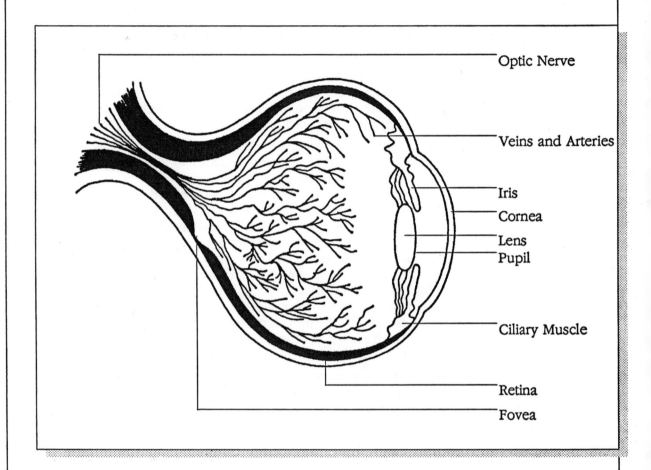

Optic Nerve

Veins and Arteries

Iris

Cornea

Lens

Pupil

Ciliary Muscle

Retina

Fovea

The Iris and Pupil

The iris is the colored membrane between the cornea and the lens. From a vision fitness perspective, the muscle of the iris is stimulated by the absence or presence of light. When there's plenty of light, this muscle causes the pupil (black aperture in the center of the iris) to get smaller. In the dark, the pupil gets larger.

Since we're discussing how the iris regulates the amount of light entering the eye, let's review the value of full-spectrum sunlight. There is a growing body of evidence that the light that enters your eyes, especially natural sunlight, plays an important role in balancing your nervous system. Contrast your typical day with that of your native African counterpart. You use electric or fluorescent light sources; you also look through windows, car windshields, eyeglasses, and contacts, which absorb some of the near ultraviolet rays of sunlight. The effect on the body is equivalent to using multi-vitamin supplements but leaving out B complex. Your nervous system has to adjust for the loss of the near ultraviolet.

This compensation disturbs the natural balance of the body and ultimately the organ structures, including the eyes. On the other hand, because your African counterpart spends much time out of doors, his or her eyes can absorb the full range and amount of sunlight the body will need.

According to John Ott, reporting in his book entitled *Light, Radiation and You*, it's the presence of full-spectrum light that permits maximum narrowing of the pupil. When devices that absorb the near ultraviolet are worn, he says, a larger pupil is measured. For many years my colleague, Dr. Raymond Gottlieb, and I have hypothesized that having enlarged pupils on a chronic basis may predispose certain persons to glaucoma. In fact, for patients who have been diagnosed as having a buildup in pressure behind the eye (glaucoma), a medication that reduces the pupil size is routinely prescribed. The wider the pupil, the more likely pressure behind the eye builds up due to a blockage of the flow of fluids. Why not consider enjoying sunlight and naturally accomplishing the same effect as the medication? In consultation with an ophthalmological colleague, some of my patients with "thin-angle" glaucoma have been able to reduce their medications as their vision fitness developed. (It is imperative that you first communicate with your ophthalmologist before reducing medications.)

I suggest spending 20 minutes or so per day outside (in rainy Oregon this is not always possible!) aiming your head toward the sun, eyes closed. Feel the warmth on your face. Imagine a packet of warm energy entering through your closed eyelids, striking the iris. Feel the pupil closing down. Visualize how small it is. Give a blink and let the pupil get smaller when the light enters the eye. After the blink, imagine the pupil getting bigger.

Begin slowly moving your chin toward your left shoulder and then to the right shoulder, breathing deeply and occasionally blinking. If the sunlight is too intense, spend more time with the eyes closed before blinking. If you notice a tendency to close one eye more than the other in sunlight, this may further confirm a lack of vision fitness in terms of how the two eyes work together as a team. This exercise will be described in more detail in Chapter 12.

Another suggestion: See if you can reduce the need to wear sunglasses. If you ski, or for occupational reasons need to wear sunglasses, obtain a neutral grey tint, polaroid, or Rayban G15 tint. Speak to your optometrist or optician. Your sight is worth wearing a high-quality lens that you can be sure will absorb the undesirable short ultraviolet frequency of light in those specialized situations. Full-spectrum lighting is available in fluorescent tubes. For incandescent lighting, use a daylight blue color-corrected bulb (see Products For Seeing Beyond 20/20).

The Lens and Ciliary Muscle

The lens is a transparent convex-shaped structure that focuses the light entering through the pupil to form an image on the retina. The ciliary muscle governs the focusing of the eye by changing the shape of the lens. This "focusing" muscle is thought by most to be an involuntary muscle (not under one's voluntary control). This means that if you overfocus, your ciliary muscle can become cramped and sluggish. You'll then notice blurriness when looking at near objects and/or far distances. You may also observe your speed of focusing to be slower.

However, stimulation of the ciliary muscle produces more power in the focusing ability of the lens. This in turn permits you to focus on small details at closer distances, as when reading, sewing, crocheting, doing computer work, finding numbers in the phone book, and so on.

In order to maintain focusing fitness, then, every few minutes glance up at a far object and bring it quickly into focus. Put your thumb up at about six inches from your eyes. Focus on your thumbnail, then look off into the distance, and then focus back onto your thumb. When looking up close, remember to breathe in.

When you drive, "zoom" your focus to different objects—for example, the rearview mirror, dashboard, license plate of the car in front of you, window, and then side mirror. Repeat the cycle as many times as you want. While on the phone, focus on the receiver, objects on your desk, out the window, back to your pen, and so on. Keep the eyes moving, focusing to different distances, and your focusing muscle will be flexible and fit.

Retina and Fovea

The retina is the light-sensitive membrane lining the inner eyeball at the back of the eye. Light energy striking the retina is converted into chemical signals that carry the information via the optic nerve to the brain. The retina serves to detect movement in one's peripheral (side) vision and permits night vision.

The most acute visual perception—20/20 vision—takes place at a small area near the center of the retina called the fovea centralis. When entering rays of light all focus clearly on the fovea, you'll see 20/20.

The danger in trying to see clearly is that you might strain your eyes. Avoid staring at one place for an extended period. Let your eyes dance and move. Staring leads to an overstimulation of the fovea, and possible cramping of the focusing muscle. In turn, this can result in less effective functioning of the retina, which means you'll miss some objects in your peripheral vision. When you are too focused (foveal), your vision fitness percentage will also decrease. Simply put, you'll notice less in your environment. It's almost like being too self-focused.

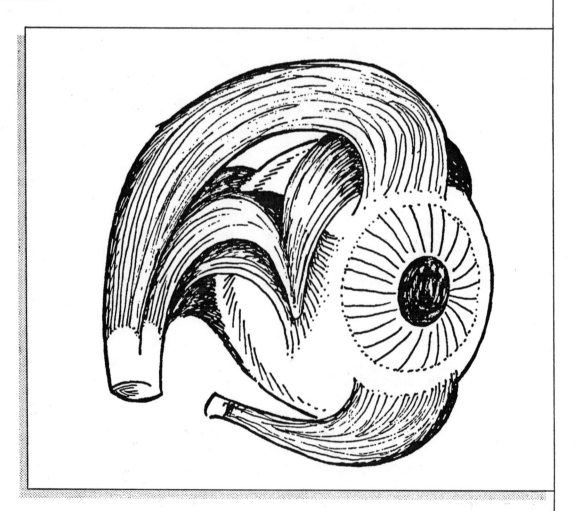

The solution here is to emulate the way your African counterpart vigilantly scans his environment. Keep the eyes moving so that the fovea is constantly receiving new stimulation. Blink and breathe.

Outside Muscles of the Eye

In order for the eyes to be able to move in myriad directions, each eye has six muscles surrounding the eyeball. The eyes can move up, down, left, right, inward and outward, always paralleling each other. The muscles are attached to the white of the eye, called the sclera. The question is, how skillful are you in coordinating these muscle movements? This will greatly determine your level of vision fitness.

Recall that the muscles of the eyes are very strong. In order to preserve vision fitness, stretching or warming up these muscles is suggested. Sounds like an aerobic warm-up, doesn't it! Seat yourself comfortably, with your hands supported and both feet firmly on the ground. You can choose between keeping the eyes open or closed. Take a few deep breaths. When ready, with the next breath, stretch your eyes as high as they can go without straining. Hold the breath, and when ready to exhale, stretch the muscles into the extreme downward position and breathe out.

Repeat the up and down movement for three breaths, and then do the left and right directions. Then up to the right and down to the left, and finally, up to the left and down to the right. If you feel any residual tension in the muscles, extend the breath slightly and reduce the degree of stretching. Avoid straining or extreme stretching. Remember, vision fitness develops while exercising in a relaxed way. After a fitness procedure like "muscle stretching," try a "cooling off" period. Rub your hands together and gently cover your closed eyes with the palms of your hands. Overlap the fingers above the bridge of your nose to create as much darkness as possible. Keep the eyes covered for one or two minutes or 20 to 50 breaths. You'll not only be relaxing the eyes, but you'll probably experience quietness of the mind. This is like meditation for the eyes.

When you remove your palms, you'll observe colors much brighter, see more contrast, and enjoy a wonderful, relaxed feeling in your eyes and brow muscles. Observe whether or not your vision fitness percentage has changed.

Here's another useful exercise: Learn to turn the eyes in, crossing them. (No, they won't get stuck, even if your mother said they would.) Attempt to look at the bridge of your nose. If it's too difficult, use a thumb. Slowly bring the thumb toward your nose and feel the eye muscles pulling in. These inner recti muscles are the turning-in muscles. This turning-in is vitally important for efficient and prolonged reading. If the inner recti don't coordinate well, the eyes will rely on the ciliary (focusing) muscle instead, and this could result in a focusing muscle spasm and blurring. So there is a connection between the turning-in of the eyes and focusing. Have someone check that your eyes are turning in equally. Breathe in as you move your thumb toward your nose. Breathe out as you zoom your looking to a faraway object. Make sure your shoulders and body muscles are relaxed.

Practice this fitness exercise every day for 10 to 20 breaths. You can remove your eyeglasses for these fitness routines. If you're a contact lens wearer and can remove them, do so; otherwise, leave them in.

One further suggestion: Spend time studying the diagrams of the eyes and progress to the point where you can visualize the eye structures with your eyes closed. Then when you stretch the eye muscles, or zoom back and forth, or do other eye exercises, blink and breathe, and visualize the particular portion of your eye's anatomy that's being stimulated. Picturing the part being trained will improve your performance of the exercises and further enhance your overall vision fitness.

Observe that these vision fitness exercises take minimal time to implement. Your eyes serve you well; love them, exercise them, and maintain their vision fitness.

SUMMARY

EYE ANATOMY	VISION FITNESS EXERCISE
Cornea	Blinking every three seconds
Iris muscles/Pupil	Using full-spectrum lighting; exposing closed eyes to sunlight and blinking
Lens/Ciliary muscle	Breathing; zooming (near/far focusing)
Retina/Fovea	Non-staring; moving the eyes frequently
Eye muscles	Eye muscle stretching
Overall eye/mind relaxation	Palming the eyes
Overall eye fitness	Visualizing the parts of the eye while exercising

5. BEING AND SEEING OR DOING AND LOOKING

When thinking of being and doing, and how these states relate to vision, I am reminded of the movie *The Gods Must Be Crazy*. A Bushman in Southern Africa, while one day minding his own business (being), is suddenly confronted with a Coca-Cola bottle that has been dropped out of a small airplane flying above. The Coca-Cola bottle triggers many events that shift the Bushman's state from being to doing. Our Bushman's formerly peaceful lifestyle becomes filled with anxiety, aggressiveness, and movement at a faster pace. As the bottle is explored by the tribe members, social interaction among the Bushmen also changes.

The non-Coca-Cola Bushman typifies being. Most forms of relaxation, such as aerobic exercise, meditation, biofeedback, yoga, tai chi and Feldenkreis, produce a bodily state associated with being. This quiet, gentle, calm state is associated with seeing. When you are being, there's very little thinking or understanding. You are, via your eyes, more connected to the world around you. Visually, you can think of being as seeing with the retina. You see everything, but don't pay attention to any one particular detail.

Doing, on the other hand, is related to looking. Can you imagine being the Bushman and suddenly having to determine the meaning of a Coca-Cola bottle? The bottle brought up all kinds of questions for the Bushman. Where did it come from? Was this a sign that the gods were angry? It even affected the traditional social interactions of the Bushman tribe. They became competitive and began fighting for the bottle—more doing! Doing is associated with thinking, questioning, analyzing, and looking for the details. As you can appreciate, doing may be thought of as looking with the fovea of the eye.

In our Western culture the environmental stimulation of television, automobiles, busy downtowns, schedules, going to school, financial pressures, and being busy all promotes a doing state. Scientific inquiry in medicine, science, mathematics, and other forms of research all requires doing.

If you spend too much time looking (doing), then you promote a more foveal point of view, which in turn promotes overfocusing. This overfocusing first begins in the mind (mental focus), which later leads to overstraining of the ciliary muscle (eye focus). At this point you'll become aware of a drop in vision fitness such as blurring, eye fatigue, double vision, or staring.

Visually speaking, then, your fovea is overused in our modern world. This is one of the ways your natural vision fitness drops off. When there's an imbalance between the doing and being activities in your life, an imbalance occurs in the brain. The vision fitness approach calls for you to become aware of those times when you feel the imbalance between doing/looking and being/seeing.

Let's use the example of your reading a book. It's after dinner, you feel perfectly relaxed. You're sitting in your favorite chair, the lighting is good. After about 30 minutes you catch yourself bringing the book closer to your eyes. Over time the distance between the book and your eyes closes down to six to eight inches.

You also feel a little tension in the neck. What started off as a balanced doing/ being activity moved to a doing task. The unconscious staring and "hard" focusing of the ciliary muscle produced a shift in energy flow from the brain. The reduced reading distance and neck tension was feedback from your body and eyes that your mind and eye muscles became tense. You became too foveal!

Other situations when this can occur include watching television, working at a computer terminal, sewing, and similar near-oriented work. Notice if your legs become tired or tense. Are they crossed? Are you frowning or squinting your eyes? After these kinds of activities, do your eyes feel heavy or ache? The classic indicators of movement from a being to a doing state are staring, shallow breathing, and non-blinking. Periodically check your posture, breathing, blinking, and your working distance.

What Is Your Visual Style?

The being/doing concept, as it relates to vision fitness, is associated with your visual style. You have acquired ways of looking at—or alternatively, seeing— situations in your life. The following exercise will assist you in determining your visual style. Do you favor looking or seeing? Circle those behaviors* that apply to you.

*Some of these behaviors were shared by Optometrist Dr. Richard Kavner through personal correspondence.

BEING/SEEING VISUAL STYLE:

a) Better reading scores than math scores.

b) Lose place when reading or writing ideas.

c) Not precise with language or ideas.

d) Distractable, impulsive, fast but imprecise when performing detailed tasks.

e) Tendency for mind to drift, day dreaming, or "spacing out."

f) Tendency to work from general to specific.

g) More difficulty driving in p.m. than a.m., difficulty maintaining attention in detailed tasks.

h) Inability to sustain near-distance work; tend to get sleepy.

i) Difficulty in concentrating on continued events, like a lecture.

j) Tired to the point of irritability when you get home from work.

DOING/LOOKING VISUAL STYLE:

a) Not always aware of overall picture or end result of action.

b) Tend to get caught up in projects and details.

c) More often precise and slow in tasks requiring a broad understanding.

d) Difficulty shifting attention from task to task, idea to idea.

e) Feel that you must finish the present task before starting another.

f) Difficulty pulling out into traffic.

g) Dislike ambiguity (for example, situations involving contradictions).

h) People say you tend to be "too" logical and analytical.

i) Give the impression of being a "know-it-all."

j) Tendency not to notice things outside the immediate field of vision.

Add the number of behaviors that you have circled for each of the two categories. Optimally, there should be an equal number for doing and being. If this is not so, which behaviors would you like to acquire or eliminate? Become aware of situations in your life that involve those desirable or undesirable behaviors. For example, if you find yourself rushing through a project and making careless mistakes, are you not focusing enough, i.e., doing? If so, how would you prefer to be performing at that moment? Find the vision fitness exercise—most likely zooming, breathing, crossing your eyes, or palming—that will restore the balance between looking and seeing.

To further appreciate this doing/looking and being/seeing concept, some understanding of the brain is helpful. The brain has two hemispheres. In most people the left brain can be thought of as performing the mathematical, speech, logical, analytical, linear, and rhythmical functions. The right brain, for most, is the seat of creative, artistic, musical, expansive, and feeling functions.

Ideally, we use both hemispheres, switching back and forth. It seems that if we could separate the hemispheres, however, each part has the following special qualities.

QUALITIES

"Left Brain"	"Right Brain"
linear	spatial
orderly	random
objective	subjective
analytical	intuitive
mathematical	artistic
verbal	feeling (emotions)
logical	sensing
temporal (time)	spatial
detailed	whole (gestalt)
physical	creative
differentiated	undifferentiated

From a vision fitness perspective, I propose that the fovea (looking) triggers off a left-brain mode of processing (doing). In a looking mode or doing state, there will be a tendency for you to be more time-oriented, logical, and verbal. You will also tend to be more linear in your thinking; you will tend to be focused on one line of thought. From videotaped clinical observations of my patients' faces, I have noted more tension in and around the eye muscles and face while they are looking. You can learn to recognize your own shift to the doing/looking state by noticing times when your breathing becomes shallow, you stare, and you produce tension in the eye muscles, neck, and shoulders.

When you are unable to stay focused (foveal) and you tend to be "spacey," you're swinging the balance over to the being side. Probably at that point you're tending to be more retinal than foveal. This is akin to being more intuitive. Activities like art, music, dancing, drawing, and some sports promote a state of being, that is, seeing.

There is a danger when we attempt to tackle activities that promote retinal seeing (accessing right-brain) in a left-brain way. Right-brain activities tend to be fun, light, and are recreational. Being left-brain, analyzing, trying to work it out can take away the "lightness" of playing a musical instrument, dancing, participating in a sport, painting, and doing photography. The visual danger, at a physical level, is that the eyes will tend to be too foveal when we behave in a left-brained way. This will promote a drop in natural vision fitness. However, the competitive nature promoted in our culture—group sports, making good grades in school, the business world, and keeping up with the neighbors are examples—tends to advance more doing even while participating in being activities. So whatever you are doing check for shallow breathing, staring, and having tension in the eyes. Zoom, and let your eyes dance—the being state will be re-activated.

Improving your vision fitness involves teaching your brain and your eyes to maintain an optimum working relationship. Being while doing, or seeing while looking, is what produces high-level vision fitness. The vision fitness lenses mentioned in Chapter 3 will assist you in achieving this balance. As mentioned, the slight blur leads to foveal as well as retinal stimulation. Some of you might shift back to doing/looking and find this 16 percent blur uncomfortable.

You can now understand how using vision fitness lenses can alter your control of the brain's hemispheres. I believe that 20/20 lenses tend to generate a more left-brain/doing state. You may notice your desire to talk and explain more (left-brain) when wearing 20/20 lenses. On the other hand, vision fitness lenses permit you to be with the world; you will tend to think less but observe and see more.

Recall the eye anatomy and vision fitness exercise chart in Chapter 4. Breathing, blinking, zooming, eye crossing, palming, and using full-spectrum lighting are vision fitness exercises that can help you to restore a being state while doing. Chapter 12 is designed for you to explore this further. Enjoy being balanced— look and see!

6. NUTRITION AND AEROBICS FOR YOUR EYES

The level of vision fitness in your eyes can only be as good as the quality of fuel you provide to them and the efficiency of those muscles and organs that play a role in circulating blood flow to them. It would be easy if the eyes had a separate mouth and you could feed them lots of carrots or other specialized vision-enhancing foods. However, since one mouth serves the whole body, the probability is very high that what you eat will ultimately affect the eyes. Exercising the major body muscles will obviously affect the blood flow and thus nutrients traveling to the eye structures.

To simplify complex topics like nutrition and body exercise, I suggest you recall our native African. I am not saying we should return to the life of a Bushman, but to recognize the value of treating our bodies with the same care and respect as he does. The Bushman metaphor continues to be valid especially since most of them have excellent vision. Consider his typical day: Awakening in his primitive hut, he might light a fire (the really primitive African might rub two sticks together) and embark on a one-mile walk to bring enough fresh water to prepare a warm drink for his family. Part of the trip might be spent running, and on the return trip, the water would be carried on his head or around his neck. Food preparation could involve hunting in sunlight, using his eyes and many of his body muscles. Food consumption is simple—berries, fruit, a little meat, vegetables, beans, and grains. Time is spent preparing the food and savoring the taste over a lengthy meal with other family members. There's a natural balance of aerobic exercise and small portions of healthy food.

Contrast that lifestyle to a typical scenario in your Western form of lifestyle. You are awakened by an alarm clock when it's still probably dark. After rolling out of bed you exercise your finger muscle by switching on the light. Programmed from the night before, the coffee machine has your pick-me-up waiting. You shave (if you do) with an electric razor or you breathe in the chemical fumes of shaving cream as it prepares your stubble for its removal. With a flick of a handle, hot water pours out from the shower. After dressing, you select a prepared cereal (usually with added sugar and salt), add milk that you bought at a store, and eat a meal, probably while standing. You exercise by walking to your car, train, or bus, in which you travel to your place of work. The point is that your modern lifestyle might have a bearing on the maintenance and development of your vision fitness.

While researching the effects of nutrition and exercise on vision fitness, I subjected myself and other volunteers to many experiments. The results clearly suggest that you can monitor your looking and seeing fitness by the type of food you eat and the extent of aerobic exercise you perform. During our original research study in 1982, for example, one of the subjects reported a nutrition-related experience he had during the 21-day experimental period. We had all participants eliminate red meat, alcohol, sugar, and dairy and processed foods. They ate fresh fruits and vegetables with a minimum of chicken and fish. Soy products, beans, and grains were encouraged.

> Eric was following the program very effectively. He hadn't worn his strong eyeglasses for eight days, had given up all coffee and sugar, and his natural vision fitness level had improved by 30 percent. One night he and his wife went to dinner and Eric succumbed to a cup of coffee and a delicious piece of cheese-cake. Within 30 minutes Eric's vision fitness had dropped sufficiently so that his wife had to lead him by the arm from the restaurant.

From the evidence I've seen in the literature (see Appendix references) and my communication with researchers around the world, it would appear that the ciliary (focusing) muscle is sensitive to fluctuations in blood sugar levels. I recall a 14-year-old who was learning to use natural vision fitness, thus avoiding strong eyeglasses. Her natural vision fitness was 76.5 percent. One day Pat arrived at the clinic, where I was conducting vision fitness training and research, with a soda pop. Before she was able to drink her pop, I recorded her natural vision fitness level with both eyes open. I then asked her to drink the soda. Within 15 minutes, there was a significant decrease in her vision fitness to 58.5 percent.

Another participant during the research of the vision fitness approach shared the following experience:

> "For over a week I had restricted my eating to rice, vegetables, a small portion of fish or chicken, fresh fruit, yogurt, and bread. I walk to work and each day, through my vision fitness lenses (83.6 percent), I could see objects, signs, and cars a lot clearer. On the ninth day of the experiment, I stopped into a fast-food place. After consuming scrambled eggs and a roll, I continued the walk to my office. Within 20 minutes, I could hardly see through my reduced power lenses. I would estimate my vision fitness dropped to 70 percent. This experience convinced me that what I eat affects my looking."

These kinds of reports are very common. The intake of certain foods by sensitive individuals seems to cause an allergic reaction that can be revealed in the functioning of the eye. It would seem that these foods trigger a chemical change that is recorded by the eyes.

Another factor may also be at work. Your eyes are located very far from vital organs like the heart, lungs, liver, and kidneys. However, if these organs are forced to overwork due to consumption of unsuitable foods, then your eyes will bear the consequences. For example, the liver purifies the blood before it carries off the nutrients to the different parts of the body. If you consume fatty foods then the liver has to overwork, and some remaining debris might end up in the blood that ultimately reaches the eye. In a sense, the eye vessels and parts can be thought of as a dumping ground. The eye will only be as healthy as the content and purity of the blood.

Exercise, particularly an aerobic variety, allows your heart to pump more blood through the different parts of the body. The blood in the eyes has a chance to be flushed, which stimulates the eyes during and after exercise. The nerves are also then better able to send fast and accurate messages.

Over the years, I have received reports from my patients about changes in their vision fitness percentage while involved in aerobic activity. Long-distance runners have reported periods of intense clarity without lenses. Students already having a natural 100 percent vision fitness percentage relate how much more they can retain while reading after an aerobic workout. Video display terminal operators who exercise at lunch time have experienced less eyestrain by the end of the day compared to days when they don't exercise.

A report from a professional tennis player who completed a vision fitness program further illustrates the point:

> "Exercise for me is a form of expanding my rhythm (breath) and space occupied by my body. As I stretch my body and eye muscles into space, so my ability to see increases. While exercising, I move my eyes left, right, up, and down. I focus to different distances.
>
> Whenever possible, I wear no lenses while playing; otherwise I slip on my vision fitness prescription. I have on a number of occasions beaten my partner using my natural vision fitness. It's almost like I can see the moving ball better.
>
> My warm-up procedure includes swinging my body from left to right, hanging my head down, and rolling my neck. These exercises help me loosen my muscles and keep them flexible. I also monitor my breathing and stretch my eyes. After a vigorous workout, I'll palm my eyes for 50 breaths and visualize the eye parts receiving healthy blood."

We've seen how our Bushman incorporates natural practices of good eating and exercising into his daily schedule. What about your own lifestyle? In the past you've probably been too busy doing to make room for similar practices in your routine. But what we've learned about vision fitness makes it all the more important that you pay careful attention to the foods you choose to eat and set aside time to exercise.

Well Then, What Should I Eat?

This is a very complex question. I wish there was a simple formula I could give you. Probably the most effective way for me to make suggestions is to share with you my personal experiences and experiments. Over the years, I have studied different nutritional approaches to better my own chances for disease prevention, and also to increase my vision fitness. What follows is my personal approach to eating. It is an assimilation of many theories and practical experiences. Before I begin, I'll relate two perspectives that allowed me to be more flexible.

A macrobiotic teacher from Japan one day said to me:

> "**If** you cannot occasionally drink beer or eat red meat, then your body is sick."

The other perspective was shared by a cancer patient participating in a natural approach to cancer treatment. When questioned about the nutritional approach that contributed to his cancer regression, the man stated:

> "**I** eat anything my body wants. When I eat an ice cream sundae, I tell my body to really enjoy the value of this food."

What then, is my philosophy regarding food? I believe in moderation. I prefer a non-fanatical approach to well-being. Preparing even the simplest meal is like creating a work of art. Eating for me is a joy. Food to me is sacred. I also feel that if I am in tune with my body, it'll let me know what food it desires. Of course, I have to monitor what is emotional gratification versus nutritionally sound principles.

I do the best I can to avoid producing new belief systems about foods. An example would be a report I read that an overconsumption of dairy products can lead to a change in the metabolism of the lens of the eye. This may later result in a cataract (clouding of the lens). Based on this report, it would be very easy to tell you to eliminate dairy products from your diet. Other research states that excessive sugar and simple carbohydrate intake is bad for the ciliary (focusing) muscle. Do I then suggest giving up sugar? I would prefer that you experiment for yourself. I have found that some dairy products and sugar are okay for myself; however, do you know what your tolerance is? Do you know the critical point that will lead to a decrement in vision fitness?

With this in mind, here is my own dietary approach: I make use of grain (rice, millet, quinoa, and buckwheat) and legume (bean) combinations as my staple diet. I add soy and other bean products like tofu and tempeh. I add sea vegetables to my grains and soups, and use miso (soy bean paste) at least twice a week as a soup or drink. Chicken and fish, once a week, are supplemented with steamed, pressure cooked, or stir fried vegetables that include the deep root variety like daikon. I use small amounts of fresh ginger, garlic, and cayenne powder, and other seasoning herbs. I have a fresh salad with live sprouts like alfalfa.

My liquid intake includes herb teas, vegetable drinks, and fresh extracted juice from fruit (summertime) and vegetables. I eat fruit and drink juices mainly in the summer months. Breads, soy margarine, and homemade preserves are used as special treats.

For breakfast I use a mixed grain cereal with soy or skim milk. When eating breakfast out, usually once every other week, I'll order scrambled, poached, or soft-boiled eggs and whole-wheat toast. When eating other meals out, I'll order wine or beer and have fresh fish. Occasionally, I'll have a dessert.

When I notice a drop in my vision fitness, I'll take a multivitamin and mineral supplement and include extra ascorbate vitamin C, multi B, a water soluble A and amino acid chelated zinc. (See Products For Seeing Beyond 20/20.)

In summary, consider the basics. Remember the four food groups. Cut back a little on dairy products and red meat and balance the groups.

Most important: Using a vision fitness lens and making use of the biofeedback nature of the eyes, you can monitor which foods affect you. Recall that the effects may be more than just a drop in your vision fitness percentage. You may experience impaired "two-eyed fitness" (ability of the two eyes to work together). Also, your looking/seeing balance may be upset. But in time and with patience you'll begin to know what your body desires for maximimum general and vision fitness.

How Much Should I Exercise?

As a rule of thumb, exercise for 15 to 20 minutes while the pulse beats between 125 and 145 beats per minute. Again, moderation is the key. A slight perspiration is satisfactory, but don't be so tired that you're panting.

While exercising, get in touch with a balance between your being and doing. Your seeing can become more vivid. Your field of vision may widen and colors become brighter. You may feel as if there is nothing in your way. Your body can feel expansive and open.

Experiment and discover what happens for you with each lifestyle change you make. Nurture your body with good foods and healthy exercise, and your vision will be fit.

THE NUTRITIONAL ELEMENTS AND THEIR EYE RELATIONSHIP

EYE ANATOMY	NUTRITIONAL ELEMENTS
Sclera (white of eyeball)	Calcium
Conjunctiva (covering of sclera)	Vitamins B_2, B_{12}, folic acid
Cornea	Vitamin A
Lens	Vitamins C, E, B_2
Ciliary Muscle	Chromium
Retina	Vitamin A; zinc and other minerals
Area around the Fovea (Macula)	Vitamin B complex

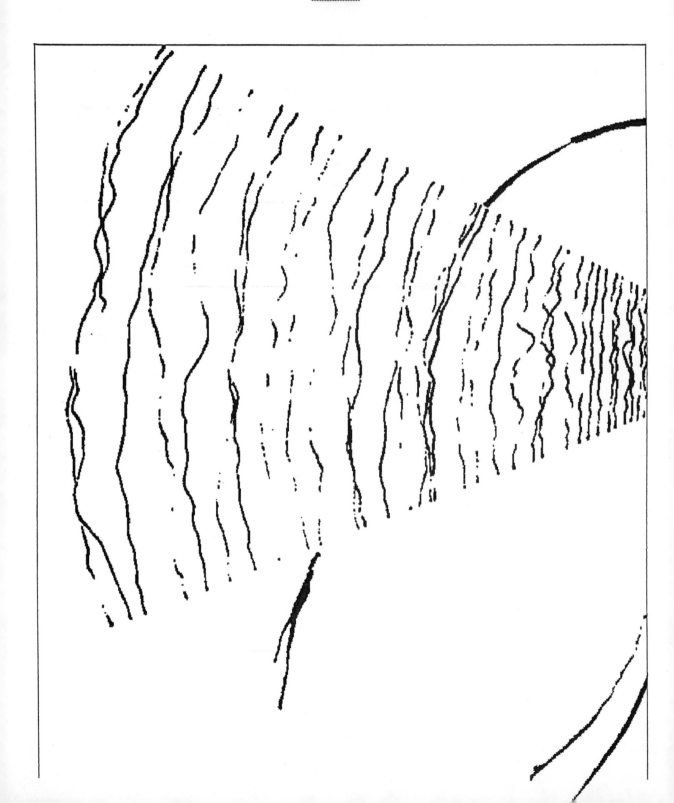

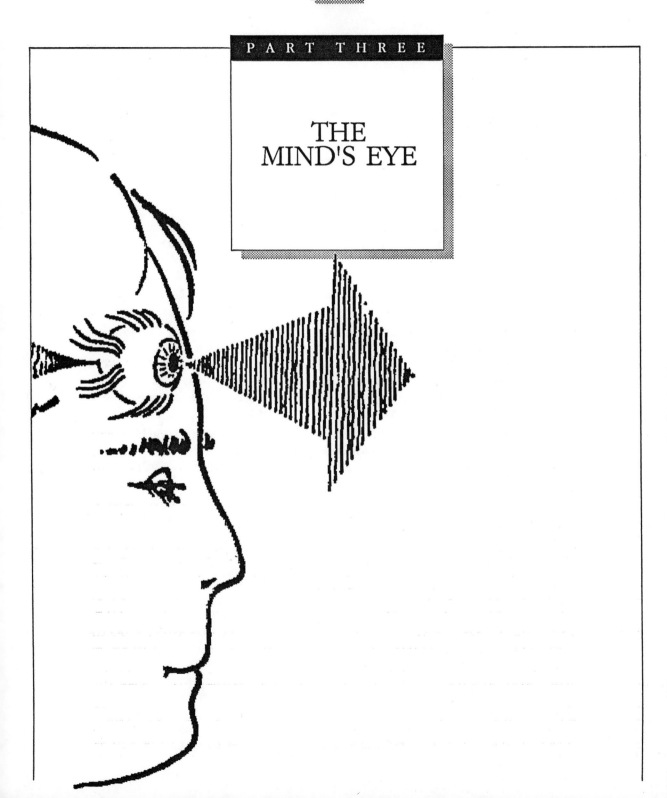

PART THREE

THE
MIND'S EYE

7. DOES YOUR INNER VISION GUIDE YOUR OUTER SEEING?

To answer this question you might find it helpful to transcend your traditional view of your eyes—that they're bad, there's a problem, or you can't see. Attempt to keep an open mind. Begin using the ideas that follow in a self-experiment. In the beginning, your rational mind may wish to dismiss these ideas as impossible. Ask that part of you to be patient. Be open.

> The best and most beautiful things in the world cannot be seen or even touched. They must be felt with the heart.
> —Helen Keller

Since the time you stood in line for your eye test at school, you've thought that your eyes are either good or bad. If you "failed" the school eye test, you were told to see an eye doctor. The doctor probably told you that your eyes were weak, long, short, cloudy, or had too much pressure. Blurriness, double vision, eyestrain, cataracts, glaucoma, iritis, nearsightedness, and the other eye conditions may have been involved in the diagnosis.

Your mother, father, or other family members probably comforted you by saying that you got their "weak" eyes. In your mind's eye you elaborated the "problem" by agreeing that your eyes were weak. Each visit to the eye doctor, for most of you, meant further bad news. Your eyes needed a stronger lens prescription, surgery, or medications. So the process continued and the belief about your eyes became further ingrained. Could it be that this thinking contributed to the decreased capability of the physical eye to do its job?

Back to your native African counterpart. In the middle of the jungle there are no optometrists or ophthalmologists. If and when the jungle-dweller experiences a "problem" with his eye, like a sore, puffiness, redness, or blurred or impaired vision, he visits the local medicine man or shaman. Rather than only obtaining a cure, the "patient" is encouraged to explore why the gods or spirits are making his eye the way it is. In a sense, the shaman acts as a teacher by helping the person to determine the cause of the condition. For example, redness with swelling may metaphorically be associated with inner anger or upset. A ritual might follow. Perhaps a natural concoction from vegetation, animal juices, and soil (what we call a poultice) will be given to the African to place on the eye(s). The healing process includes the "patient" as an active participant by having him look at his involvement in the eye condition. This approach goes beyond simply treating the symptom or even clearing up the physical condition.

Drawing on this metaphor, you can begin to think of your eye condition as a computer printout revealing the mind's eye. I believe that the present condition of the eye reflects past mind's-eye pictures of how you saw parts of your world and life. It's a combination of your thoughts, beliefs, fears, and angers. It also includes perceptions picked up from your parents, siblings, teachers, etc. This is why you don't all develop similar eye conditions. Each of you carries your own unique imprint of past patterns of perception. You visit your traditional eye doctor with a symptom—perhaps blurriness, eyestrain, "floaters," or pain. Your eye doctor examines the eyes and takes various measurements. He then makes a comparison to some norm and informs you whether or not you fit into that norm. If you don't, then some remedial measures, not substantially different from the African ritual, may be suggested. These usually take the form of eyeglasses, contact lenses, surgery, or medications.

Contrast this familiar approach with that of the modern preventive eye doctor, usually a functional optometrist. Like the shaman, he or she views the physical eye as a mirror of the mind's eye. In effect, the eye condition reveals something about your inner perception, either current or from the past.

The obvious and ideal situation would be to combine the traditional Western and shamanistic approaches. Firstly, you can use the technology of a vision fitness lens prescription. Secondly, you can enlist your eye doctor, or a suitably trained professional, to assist you in looking at the types of perceptions you have in your mind's eye.

A couple of case examples will bring this more into focus for you.

Annie at age 41 claimed to be bored with life, detaching herself from the world by living in a small cabin in the central Oregon woods. I observed her as a "sweet," slightly built woman. By isolating herself in the woods, Annie avoided seeing herself in relation to the rest of the world. She had withdrawn from traditional life, to learn about another part of her being. It was no surprise when she described her physical "ailments." Annie had been a diabetic, under control for many years. (Am I "sweet" enough—liked and accepted as I am?) The foveal area of both retinas had become detached, impairing the retina's function. This resulted in her side vision becoming quite narrow. Behaviorally speaking, Annie had secluded her mind's-eye seeing, and detached her willingness to see and clearly participate in life.

I assisted Annie in correlating these observations, and following our first visit she went for eye surgery. Having the new awareness helped Annie to change her vision of her lifestyle. In a way her mind's eye was retrained to perceive in harmony with the reality seen by the physical eye.

Obviously, this is an extreme example of the proposition that the mind's eye can influence the physical eye. I didn't expect Annie to recover much of her vision fitness. However, she moved from a position of despair—one of believing she was going to go blind—to a new outlook that enabled her to go back to a small town and successfully continue a home business. Her seeing (vision) improved and the eye condition stabilized. One could speculate that the surgery alone resulted in the improved perception as well as her more positive attitude. In Annie's case her mind's eye (perspective) had been focused on the negative. The vision fitness intervention assisted her in gaining a perspective that facilitated the surgical and natural healing process.

The point is, if you believe that you have an eye "problem," then the "condition" has less chance of "getting better." In Annie's case, after our consultation, she saw her nearsighted eyes and the healing detachment "condition" as a gift. She could learn something about herself. My intensive case history and video analysis of her previous thinking and destructive inner vision pointed to her mind's-eye perceptions being one of the causes in the significant drop in vision fitness. Like the African "patient," Annie took advantage of her situation to gain new insights into how she participated in the development of the eye "gift." Also, she underwent surgical intervention to prevent the eye condition from getting worse.

Abe, age 31, had been told by his eye doctor at age 16 that by the time he was in his mid-thirties, he would need to wear eyeglasses. During his early thirties, Abe made a career change and became a computer programmer. It was at this time that he noticed blurred vision. His optometrist confirmed Abe's suspicion. His eyes were too long and thus were nearsighted. He would need moderately strong eyeglasses. During the next year Abe went through two more changes in prescription. Each time he got stronger and stronger glasses. By the third pair, Abe consulted me.

During our consultation I asked what else had been happening in his life during the career change. Eighteen months prior to getting the first pair of glasses, Abe had ended an eight-year marriage. He reported great fear and anxiety about the future. He couldn't see how he was going to make it financially. His inner vision was one of failure both in career and relationships. The intense computer study programs, Abe's memory of the eye doctor saying he would need glasses in his mid-thirties, and fear of the future all precipitated the changes in his physical eyes.

My first step was to assist Abe in changing the way he phrased things. He repeatedly used the word "can't" and the phrase "I don't know." By rephrasing to "I know," he initiated seeing in the future. For example, I would ask Abe questions like: "Where would you like to work" or "What type of relationship are you looking for?" Since Abe had internally programmed his mind's eye not to see clearly, he would respond to the question by saying "I don't know!" As long as Abe linguistically said "I don't know," his mind's eye didn't see. After a few sessions, he began to answer the above question by saying: "I would like to work for a high-tech company and I am interested in a professional woman who loves the outdoors."

These answers assisted Abe in creating clarity in his mind's eye. He had his friends remind him whenever he spoke in a negative or unaccountable way. He also used the vision fitness lenses and incorporated exercises to balance his being and doing states.

Abe very soon was able to eliminate lenses for all activities except driving. He became more outgoing and ended up finding a fabulous job and a magnificent relationship. This all happened over a seven-month period.

Each eye condition is representative of a mind's-eye perception. Also, the condition is a gift—each offers a specific lesson to learn. The following guide may help you to discover your particular gift.

EYE CONDITION OR "PROBLEM"	MIND'S EYE PERCEPTION	GIFT OR LESSON
Nearsightedness	Fear of seeing the future; pulling inward to self: "I am afraid to see what's out there."	Reach for your dream. Push outward. Learn about creating space. Confront your power.
Farsightedness	Fear of seeing the present: "I have to see out in future." Anger toward self or others. Pushing space and people away. Wanting to break out and be independent.	"Career or relationship changes may be important." Learn about commitment. Be connected to the present.
Astigmatism	Distortion of one part of your reality. Nearsightedness in one particular thread or part of your life. Restriction or fear in one of the ways you see.	Open up to the future in one area of your life. Stretch yourself beyond beliefs of what's possible in a particular part of your seeing.

Glaucoma	Feeling filled with internal pressure, like you're exploding. You're rushed. You're overly inside yourself. You're closed off.	Let go. Be free and flowing.
Macular degeneration	Loss of the central theme of life; not seeing the point to living: "Spacing out is what life's about."	Reconnect to the central focus of life.
Retinal detachment	Feeling separate, unloved. Losing touch with the outside. Not wishing to see outside your immediate line of vision.	Stay connected with others, particularly outside your immediate sphere of activity.
Cataract	Clouding or blocking out of life. You avoid seeing what there is to look at in your life.	Issues need to be looked at. Clean up the aspects of life that are clouding your view of what's important.
Eye turning	Blocking of energy. Can't-cope mechanism. Life's too much, too complicated for you to deal with.	Learn cooperation and partnership between self and the world. Accept and love self and others.
Inward	Overcompensation or excessive focusing.	Relax and look out.
Outward	Spacing out. Drifting away.	Stay centered. Focus on details.
Lazy eye	Laziness to receive or express vision. Turning off of energy. An avoidance of the truth; unacceptance.	Strive for balance. Open up to your blocks to learning in life.
Corneal conditions	Blocking off power. Fear of loss of power. Seeing pain.	Reclaim personal power and vision.

When exercising, driving your car, walking, standing in line, or before going to sleep, see all the parts of your eyes as being healthy. Use "I am" statements to affirm what you wish to see. An example could be: "I am improving my vision fitness by 10 percent in the next three weeks." Dare to dream and have a vision, whether it be healthy eyes, less eyestrain, less eyeglass dependency, a new job, a wonderful vacation, or improved natural vision fitness. Let your mind's eye orchestrate your physical eye in the direction you choose.

8. EVENTS, EXPERIENCES, AND DECISIONS: THEIR EFFECTS ON VISION

Let's again imagine you're a native African living in a jungle. Your visual world consists of a five-mile radius around your home. Since childhood you've been trained how to physically survive. You learn how to skillfully move your body, how to respond to poisonous snakes, hungry lions, and wild game you may wish to capture for food. Your physical eye has a very simplistic view of the world; it consists of the natural jungle, family members, and your home. Your mind's eye and your thinking are equally uncomplicated. Your inner perceptions of your family and surroundings are peaceful and fearless.

One day while wandering at the edge of the forest, you suddenly arrive at a new place—a view your eyes have never seen before. People with their bodies covered by clothes are driving jeeps and carrying guns. Your physical eyes send new information to your mind's eye. These new perceptions are processed in the context of your previous experiences. For example, what is your view of a gun? Since you have no previous experience, this perception will be naive. Its potential to harm is not in your visual experience. You're therefore fearless. If you then see someone being hurt by the gun, a visual fear response will be activated. When you see a gun in the future, you'll see it through filters of fear and danger.

I am sure that most of you have not lived in a secluded jungle. You have had much more exposure to events in your life that may have precipitated fear responses. I am suggesting that you've physically seen things from which your mind's eye, out of a survival instinct, has made mental decisions to protect you. Unlike the African's mind's-eye view of the world, you are exposed to one crisis or stress factor after another, including wars, television violence, hijackings, restructuring of the family unit, city life, financial challenges, competitive education, alcohol, drugs, AIDS, missing children, threats of nuclear annihilation—and the list goes on. It's not surprising that your physical eye eventually adjusts to these mind's-eye perceptions. There's potentially so much in your world today that you'd rather not see.

Before we may understand how the mind's eye can affect one's vision, we need to look more closely at how the mind's eye functions. From the moment you are conceived, even before your eyes are "seeing," your body and brain tissue store information about events. For instance, your mother eats certain foods; your body records the event via an experience. If your mother consumes too much sugar, your body experiences the sensations, and your mind's eye records and makes a decision about this experience.

After birth, your eyes begin visually capturing these events. Your mind's eye is the videotape. Stored in the brain's library is the data of all sensory experiences, that is, what you've felt, heard, said, and seen. By six months of age you were more than likely seeing 20/20; by 12 months your two eyes were working together.

Imagine for a moment that you're now 14 months old. Your attention is focused on the bright orange-red color of flames in a fireplace. You maneuver your body over to the fire and begin to play. Very soon you burn your hands and start crying. Your mind's eye records this experience of pain associated with seeing red and orange. You make a decision that red and orange is associated with pain and crying.

Later on you see some brightly colored red and orange paper. You pull away and don't wish to touch the paper, based on your previous experience. If you continue responding this way to visually presented red and orange items, the muscles and structures of your eyes learn to see in a fearful way. In effect, the eyes and your looking constrict and become tense. Because of the mind's-eye decision that red and orange burns, it sends fearful messages to the physical eye.

This is clearly evident when watching eye and facial expressions recorded by a video camera. Certain probe questions stimulate mind's-eye memories of upsetting past events. When your eyes and face are then videotaped, you'll see the tension and fear reflected in the gestures you make. It's as if your memory of the previous event triggers the survival response, and you currently see through filters of that decision. That way of seeing is then reflected in the gestures made by the eyes and face.

With this proposition in mind coupled with genetic, physical, nutritional, and environmental factors that may also have affected your eyesight, you can begin to retrace the events in your life. Did these events perhaps trigger eye and mind perceptions that brought about your present level of vision fitness? A few telling case studies will illustrate this development.

For Nancy, age 43, the first major life event she recalled was moving from town to a farm at age three. Her mother gave up a career to bring up the family and look after the home. Six months later her younger brother was born. An immediate close bond between her brother and mom developed.

During the next two years, Nancy saw her mother becoming more and more unhappy over having given up her dream to be a concert pianist. During the first grade, Nancy had a routine eye exam and everything checked out as normal. She continued to observe her mother's unhappiness at having to stay on the farm.

During the year that followed, Nancy exhibited "tomboy" behaviors. Her dad even began calling her "Billy." It was in this second-grade year that she "needed" her first pair of eyeglasses.

Between the ages of eight and 14 Nancy deeply resented the close connection between her brother and mother. She and her brother constantly fought. She experienced feelings of abandonment and began questioning whether she could trust males.

By age 12, Nancy's mother expressed the desire to leave her dad. This family change led to much confusion for Nancy, and created distortions in how she viewed relationships. During this period her eyeglasses kept becoming stronger. By age 25, Nancy married a man whom her mother disapproved of, and in the following 13 years, Nancy only saw her mother twice. At age 42, her left eye perceived significantly more "blurry" than her right eye.

When I first met Nancy she was afraid, withdrawn, and a distressed woman. During our first few sessions she correlated the above events, experiences, and internal decisions with the ways her eyes saw her parents' lives: Her nearsighted development had paralleled the events! She had seen her parents, particularly her mother, as unfulfilled. Nancy found she had replicated that perception—she lived by herself and felt lonely.

Within a few weeks Nancy began taking ownership of her life. She set new goals and dreamed new dreams, creating new mind's-eye pictures. She stimulated the physical eyes with fitness exercises and wore vision fitness lenses. Nancy realized she could stay stuck seeing the other way, as a child, or make new choices, decisions that would work for her at age 42.

When Nancy chose to change, her vision fitness began improving. At first the fitness gains were fleeting and elusive. Later flashes of clarity lasted for minutes. At times her vision fitness jumped to 95 percent through her vision fitness lenses. Other times her fitness dropped to 70 percent when she became stuck in the past. Nancy's eyes are a perfect metaphor of how one's inner vision and outer seeing/looking are connected. Nancy is still on the journey of *Seeing Beyond 20/20*, using the vision fitness lenses and participating in other personal growth experiences.

Brenda had never needed eyeglasses. When she was 19, her brother was diagnosed as having cancer and died within six months. Three months following his death, Brenda was diagnosed as nearsighted. Shortly thereafter, her right eye began turning in. She faithfully wore her new glasses thinking that her eyes would be corrected. Although her ophthalmologist suggested surgery for the turned-in eye, Brenda decided to wait. At age 21, Brenda was hired in a new job which proved to be very stressful. After eight hours of desk work, her right eye was tired and turned in even more.

Two years later, Brenda heard about the research I was conducting and asked to participate. She expressed concern that her friends at work were teasing her about her "funny" eye. The first step was to get her into vision fitness contact lenses (Brenda wouldn't wear eyeglasses). After two months of vision fitness exercises, Brenda started seeing out of both eyes for short periods of time.

One day, while learning about a particularly challenging fitness exercise, Brenda screamed out her frustration. She happened to look up at the eye chart and screamed again. Her vision fitness had increased 40 percent! Brenda then consulted a social worker with whom I was collaborating in the research. Brenda learned that she had blocked her self-expression after her brother died. She had become introverted, and difficult to be with. A further six months passed. Brenda was making steady progress; she was showing more signs of using both eyes together, her self-image was improving, and she was becoming more successful in her job. However, the pressure of work also increased. It became unbearably difficult for her to handle the teasing, when her eye did turn in. Brenda left the vision fitness program.

I met Brenda one year later. She had undergone surgery to have the right eye "straightened." Because she had the vision fitness training, both eyes were working together. As we parted, she loudly expressed herself: "...and I'm getting married next month!"

Like Nancy and Brenda, your present level of vision fitness may stem from events in your past that triggered fearful or limiting eye and mind perceptions. You can remove any "filters" you may have placed over your inner vision. As an exercise, find a quiet place where you can close your eyes. While breathing and relaxing your body parts, go back in time through the videotape library of events in your mind's eye. (An alternative exercise is to do the procedure before sleeping. Let your dreams tell you about pertinent events.) Look for events that are positive and negative. Identify experiences that may have precipitated fear responses, and mental decisions made by your mind's eye to protect you. A good rule of thumb is to look back 12 to 18 months prior to having eye symptoms or getting eyeglasses.

Record this information when you once again open your eyes. You can explore the significance of what you've seen. How do your previous mind's-eye pictures relate to your present level of vision fitness?

Now you're ready to generate new events. Have some exciting experiences so you can make new decisions about what you currently see. Make a list of recreational, work, home, family, and relationship "things" you'd like to do. Choose events that provide feelings of completion, are fun, and are different. Challenge yourself by not wearing your eyeglasses or contacts. If your vision fitness is too low, wear your vision fitness lenses. Some suggestions are:

Call your parents—say you love them!

Contact an old friend

See a good movie

Go skiing

Take sailing lessons

Plan an exciting vacation

Browse through a bookstore

Go dancing

See if you can experience each and every new event in your life as a gift. Find out what there is to learn in everything you see. Monitor your vision fitness while in each new experience. Remember to love your BLUR.

9. FEAR AND ANGER: HOW THEY AFFECT VISION

We've seen that the events, experiences, and decisions of your life (Chapter 8) are factors that can keep you from seeing as well as you otherwise would. I and other colleagues believe the common denominators responsible for the impact of these events to be fear and suppressed anger. These emotions are thought to be stored mentally in your brain, and later physically in your body. How experiencing fear and/or anger alters one's vision fitness had been difficult for me to comprehend until optometrist Robert Pepper in 1976 introduced me to the idea of working with patients on a large trampoline.

Let's imagine you are in Oregon having a session on the trampoline with me. You are wearing comfortable clothes and you remove your eyeglasses or contacts. In the center of a large room with a vaulted ceiling, you see a large trampoline. You climb up on the trampoline and begin jumping up and down, moving your arms in small circles in front of you. After a reminder, you become aware of your shallow breathing. Also, you feel how your eyes are riveted to one place. Your eye, neck, and shoulder muscles feel tight. In a real session, you might notice how the new situation produces fearful and tight feelings in your chest and stomach.

After a short while you begin mastering the trampoline bounce and you relax. You look around and notice an increase in your natural vision fitness. As you smile, you hear the next instruction: "Now do a seat drop and then a knee drop!" As before, your initial body reaction is to tighten. As you imagine doing a seat drop, you sense a fear of falling. Another response could be one of reacting: "You're crazy, I can't do that!" You are invited to observe your defensiveness and anger. You may not believe this at first. If you could imagine seeing a video recording of the trampoline session you would be convinced.

So our imaginary exercise continues, and the fear/anger pattern is repeated with each new instruction:

> "**C**ount from 1 to 10 on every bounce, and do a knee drop on 2 and a seat drop on 8."
>
> "**S**ame as before, but now clap your hands on 5 and say 'relax.'"
>
> "**N**ow go backward from 10 to 1, and let 2 become 8, 8 become 5 and 5 become 2."

Did your imaginary trampoline session produce any actual sensations of fear or anger within your body? If so, you have experienced how overload in your mind's eye produces fear. It's the fear of the unknown, of failure and rejection. In most of your life situations these fear thoughts, feelings, and the resulting muscular tensions go unnoticed. But responding in a fearful way ultimately reaches the muscles of your eyes. These muscles can spasm and become tense. Then your physical seeing is affected.

A real trampoline experience is one way to help yourself become aware of how your thoughts and feelings affect your body and especially your eyes. Then the eyes can be trained by using the vision fitness program outlined in Chapter 12. Your vision fitness percentage will later reflect this level of mastery. If you were actually to bounce up and down performing mind's-eye exercises and monitoring all the variables (on 2 do a knee drop, call out a number on every other bounce, on 5 clap your hands, on 8 do a seat drop and remember to breathe and blink), you'd find there's not enough time to think about anything but the present. Being here and now is the important variable. If you start thinking about the past or worrying about the future, your present "being" state breaks down. When this happens, your performance also breaks down. So your breakdown in performance serves as feedback, a constant reminder whenever you leave the present. Your response to these "breakdowns" lets you experience your inner fears or suppressed anger.

After four hours of actual work on a trampoline farsighted Jill, age 16, reported the following:

> "I'm amazed at how frustrated I become when I can't do something as simple as jumping up and down and spelling a word. Your reminding me to breathe and feel what's going on inside of me made me suddenly scream out, just like I want to do at my mother. After the session, I felt relieved. My body and eyes were relaxed. I could center my eyes closer to my nose and read more comfortably."

My clinical observations and personal experience of this phenomena suggest that you probably spend a lot of time examining the past in your mind's eye, looking at those old events, experiences, and decisions. You have developed a repertoire of reasons for why you are the way you are and see the way you do. It's as if your physical eye wishes to see now at your current age, but your mind's eye is still living in fear and anger about decisions made in the past. Alternatively, you spend your time worrying about how you'll do in the future.

How then can you see now? This process of staying in the present, aware of where you've been and where you are going, exemplifies the "being" state. When you relax your mind's-eye thinking and your body and eye muscles, you are more in the present. Bringing your mind's eye into the present can help you to increase your vision fitness percentage, to develop greater use of the two eyes, and to increase your memory and reading ability.

Another way to accomplish this is what Robert Pepper calls "visual mapping." In visual mapping you develop a mental plan, a strategy of what to do. Once this map is established in the mind's eye, your physical seeing can be orchestrated in a relaxed way. Take the word Louisiana. Imagine jumping on the trampoline while spelling this word without any visual map or rehearsal. If you have to think how to spell Louisiana, too much energy is put into thinking. Your attention is taken away from "being" with jumping and seeing. Then you fail to monitor your physical-eye looking in a relaxed way.

Instead, work out a visual map ahead of time. You might consider breaking up the word into three segments: (1) LOU, (2) ISI, and (3) ANA. Now with your eyes closed, imagine seeing frame (1) LOU and repeat for frames (2) and (3). When your mind's-eye picture is clear, then imagine jumping on the trampoline again. Now imagine frame (2), then (1), and finally (3). How flexible are you in manipulating three frames in your mind's eye? Feel whether or not you're straining to see.

Use the same approach with objects in your world, either without eyeglasses or while wearing your vision fitness lenses. Use the Eye-C chart (Chapter 12) in the same way. Begin allowing your mind's eye to see clearly via visual mapping. For example, picture your favorite store where you purchase fruits and vegetables. Imagine your refrigerator is empty and you're walking down the store aisles selecting juicy apples, red tomatoes, green celery, and orange carrots. See the rows of priced produce. Alternatively, while driving down the freeway see the sign for your exit clearly in your mind's eye. What is the color, shape, distance and size of the sign? Repeat the same activity using the Eye-C charts. Without straining see the edges of the letters, look at the white spaces, and from memory recall the letters. Use visual mapping to extend your visual imaginative abilities. In that way you will be developing confidence in your present seeing. That way fear and anger responses can't creep into your present. In turn, you'll stay more in the now. You'll be.

Delving into just how fear and anger are related to vision fitness brings to mind some fascinating research on multiple personalities. Researchers have found that persons with split personalities need different eyeglass prescriptions for each of their respective personalities. This means that the person's vision fitness is different for each personality state.

You might consider the vision fitness lens as a means of putting you in a different "personality state." The slight blur (16.4 percent) can in some cases frustrate you or even manifest buried fear or anger. Sometimes you may feel like you're not yourself, as if you are another person. My patients report that this way of seeing allows them to access past events and experiences in the brain (mind's eye). Many of the events have been fear-based. For example:

> George was 12 when he witnessed his brother being knocked down by a car and killed. This incident terrorized him. Approximately 12 months after the accident his eyes were measured as nearsighted. At age 25, George began a vision fitness program.
>
> At first, the physical vision fitness exercises produced relaxation of the eye muscles. Later on George noticed that after physical labor and release of physical tension, he had flashes of clear seeing.
>
> At this time George's fear of accidents and his anger toward the driver who caused his brother's death surfaced. He worked through the old feelings. Today, George can legally drive without eyeglasses and has since learned to appreciate the many gifts resulting from his brother's death.

The release of suppressed fear and anger can, indeed, allow you to experience greater vision fitness. For this stage of the vision fitness program, it is very important to have a trained person assist you. Counselors, psychologists, psychiatrists, psychotherapists, vision therapists, Bates teachers, vision educators, and rebirthers are good resources for you to use (see Resources). Let a friend be a support person as well. Keep a diary of any feelings, thoughts, dreams, or breakthroughs you have. This will be your record of your progress.

If Gerald Jampolsky's book *Love Is Letting Go of Fear* is true, then:

> "Seeing is looking with love."

10. RIGHT EYE, LEFT EYE

"**Th**e eye is wonderful; too bad there're two of them!"

More than likely you and your eye doctor assume that your two eyes will work in harmony if there is a clear image on each fovea. In my experience, this is only accurate if you're our native African, who uses his eyes in myriad ways as he moves through the jungle. The moment you tend toward left-brain central foveal looking, undue stress is created in the coordination of the two eyes. You don't use your eyes as our jungle-dweller does, so as you explore these vision fitness principles, you'll become aware that each of your eyes has a particular kind of vision.

In Chinese medicine, the right side of the body is associated with expression (left-brain control). The left side is more receiving (right-brain control). If you take this concept a step further, your right eye (I think of it as a channel) extends you, and therefore your vision, outward into the world. Your left eye receives vision information from the world. As partial evidence it's an accepted fact that each side of the face, as well as each eye, does not precisely match the other. Studying eyes and faces on video has aided me in guiding my patients to better understand the dynamics of the right eye/left eye relationship.

As an exercise, take out your contacts or remove your eyeglasses. Look out of a window at a faraway object, even if it's blurry. Keeping both eyes open, cover one eye and then the other. Repeat until you can sense whether you perceive more out of one channel than the other. Begin thinking of your eyes as a channel for energy, as if there's a laser beam traveling outward from the right eye and inward through the left eye. Notice whether you think one eye is good or bad; begin eliminating such judgments. Can you refer to your "stronger eye" as the greater perceiving channel and the other as the channel that's learning to perceive greatly? This shift in thinking will assist your mind's eye.

By now you have a sense that your perceptions are either different or equal between the two eyes. If there's a difference, you can begin exploring possible reasons why you perceive less clearly in one channel.

Some additional thoughts will help. If the left channel is connected to the right brain, then using Chinese medicine philosophy, is it possible that the left eye is the feminine eye? If so, then the way you use your left eye reflects how you see your creativity, feelings, ability to receive (love), visualizing capability, and your broad view of femininity. The opposite would be true of the right eye. How you perceive through your right eye might indicate how you see your self-expression, logic, analysis skills, intellectualizing ability, and verbal skills.

If this is true, the ramifications are phenomenal. What would happen if you covered your greater perceiving channel for a few hours per day? Would you suddenly access the fear and anger mentioned in Chapter 9? Could your looking and seeing improve? If your vision fitness did improve, would the brain qualities associated with that eye also change? Or is it the other way around—would development of the qualities associated with one side of the brain produce an increase in vision fitness in the corresponding eye? It might be that to improve your vision fitness at the level of the physical eye, you would first need to make a change in the type of thinking associated with that eye.

Beth, at age 32, was a successful attorney. During her four-year intense law school studies, which she completed at age 29, she one day noticed blurriness out of her left eye. Beth had six years previously been prescribed glasses, but only used them for movies or night driving. After consulting her eye doctor, she was told that her left eye had developed more astigmatism (unequal curvature on the cornea). Full-time use of eyeglasses was prescribed.

By the time Beth consulted me several years later, the astigmatism had worsened. Recognizing that astigmatism is a form of distortion, I assisted Beth in looking at her distortions concerning her femininity. During law school, she had been one of only three females in a class of 40. Beth felt she had been groomed to assume a masculine role as a lawyer. Beth uncovered the realization that she'd had no real model of how to be an assertive female. Instead, she had patterned herself after her male classmates. In addition, Beth's sexual preference was lesbian. In that role she also assumed being the "male."

Beth's vision fitness sessions made use of a patch over her right eye. Beth explored receiving through her left channel and expressing herself and her female qualities. Over time her vision fitness percentage improved to a level equivalent to that of age 29. As Beth developed her vision fitness, she became free of full-time use of eyeglasses. Her relationship improved and Beth reported feeling more balanced.

Let's take this idea of sexual/visual orientation a little further. Your model for being masculine in this culture is the aggressive, left-brain, intellectual, clear communicator. If you blocked or didn't accept your model of a male, namely your father, then is it possible that your right eye might reflect this as a drop in vision fitness? The left eye would reflect the opposite—your mind's-eye perceptions of your mother and your feminine viewpoint.

Now you can appreciate how essential it is that both eyes work together. The degree to which your two eyes work together, as measured by vision fitness, might reflect the masculine/feminine unification in you.

Angela was five when she and her mom first visited me. Her dad had left them when Angela was two. At age three, she developed a turning-in of the right eye. The medical diagnosis was lazy eye complicated by farsightedness. Once glasses were prescribed, the eyes looked cosmetically straight. But after a few weeks, the right eye would turn in more when her eyeglasses were removed. This continued for the next year. Angela's mother was concerned that her daughter's natural vision fitness seemed to be decreasing the more she relied on eyeglasses.

My findings confirmed this, and so I ordered a vision fitness lens prescription of 1/3 less lens power for Angela. By using advanced vision fitness exercises (see Chapter 12), Angela learned how to keep activating the foveas of both eyes. She could accomplish this to a distance of three feet with the lenses and 13 inches with her natural vision fitness (without lenses).

During the next two years, Angela and her mom periodically consulted me. During that time we uncovered deep feelings of resentment toward her dad for leaving. Also, she had few male role models who could have helped her learn how to express her own masculine side, and so she learned to suppress this maleness. Her quiet, timid, and fearful behavior reflected this imbalance.

Armed with this awareness, and the continued vision fitness exercises, her mother, teachers, and friends supported Angela in developing this part of her personality. By the time Angela reached her seventh birthday, she was able to use both eyes at all distances without lenses.The right eye hardly ever turned in. She was doing well in school and was increasingly expressive. Her mother reported that Angela was much more balanced.

To create greater balance in your own vision, consider speaking with your eye doctor about wearing a patch over your greater perceiving channel. (First read the section on patching in Chapter 12!) You can also tape a makeshift patch over the vision fitness lens corresponding to that eye. My research suggests that wearing a patch for four continuous hours is the optimum time. Of course, you should only wear the patch during non-life-threatening situations. Start off inside, doing dishes, reading, and so on. Later, venture outside. Go for a walk in a park. Many of my patients have attempted ball catching and other sports with their greater perceiving channel covered. If your vision fitness percentage is 100 percent, you can still wear the patch to emphasize the part of the brain you wish to stimulate.

Others have incorporated the vision fitness patch idea into their careers:

> Sylvia, age 44, is a pianist. Her natural vision fitness is 100 percent; however, she tends to let her right eye favor her looking. When playing the piano, Sylvia also favors her right hand. The left hand tends to push too lightly on the keyboard.
>
> After using a patch on the right eye for four hours per day during a 21-day consecutive period, Sylvia's playing significantly changed. She was more able to balance her looking between both eyes. This balance carried over to her fingers and hands. Sylvia still uses the patch whenever she feels an imbalance.

When you remove the patch, do it slowly. Light will seem quite bright. Notice the colors. Feel how great it is to once again have both eyes open. Do you now fully appreciate the value of having two eyes? You'll probably feel a lot more balance. This increased vision fitness will show up in your ability to be more effective using your eyes in work, reading, and sports. Recheck to determine whether or not the difference in perception between your two eyes has lessened. How do you feel? Record any physical or emotional responses while wearing the patch. Share your results with someone.

> "Your two eyes are wonderful!"

11. WHOLE-BRAIN PROCESSING

Whole-brain processing is your ultimate control of your mind's-eye seeing and physical looking. It's a relaxing unification of the right-eye/left-eye channels. With whole-brain processing, you accept yourself: you see your past as the preparation for where you are now; you realize that what you see now is the past reflected now. Tomorrow's vision can be anything you desire! Acknowledge your perfection and let your eyes see.

In earlier chapters you had the opportunity to relearn how to use each eye separately. You've also monitored your vision fitness in each eye. The next step is to let your brain learn how to comfortably unite the two channels. This is the highest level of vision fitness. It's the acceptance of the male and female within you. As before, whole-brain processing can be performed both at the level of your physical eye and of your mind's eye.

Physical Eye

The following vision fitness exercises will teach you to begin feeling and seeing what it's like when both eyes are working together as a team. Remember to practice the routines with minimal effort and strain. Breathing, blinking, and stretching the eye muscles still apply. In other words, don't "try" and do the exercises. Let the exercises guide you to experience the feeling of the eyes working as a team. Do changes in your thoughts, posture, the time of day, and lenses allow you to perceive differently? Use the vision fitness exercises to get to know yourself and your visual style. There's no right or wrong way to "do" the exercises. The exercises are a means for you to find out what it's like to be in a whole-brain mode of processing.

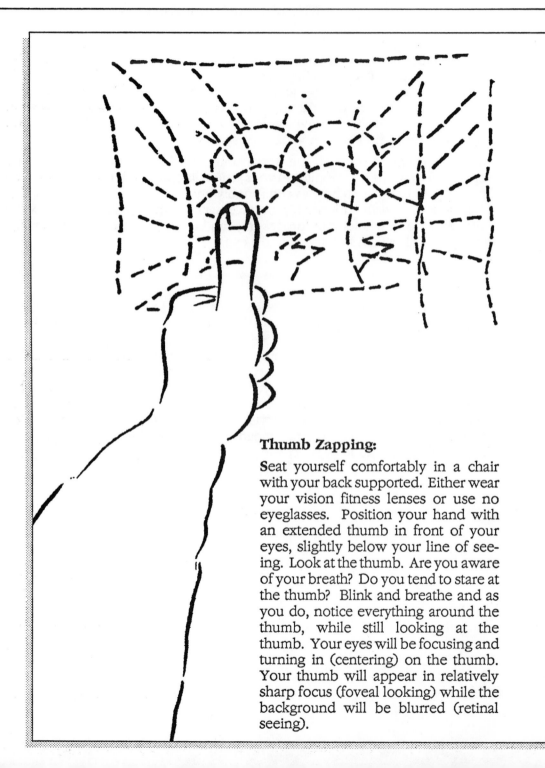

Thumb Zapping:

Seat yourself comfortably in a chair with your back supported. Either wear your vision fitness lenses or use no eyeglasses. Position your hand with an extended thumb in front of your eyes, slightly below your line of seeing. Look at the thumb. Are you aware of your breath? Do you tend to stare at the thumb? Blink and breathe and as you do, notice everything around the thumb, while still looking at the thumb. Your eyes will be focusing and turning in (centering) on the thumb. Your thumb will appear in relatively sharp focus (foveal looking) while the background will be blurred (retinal seeing).

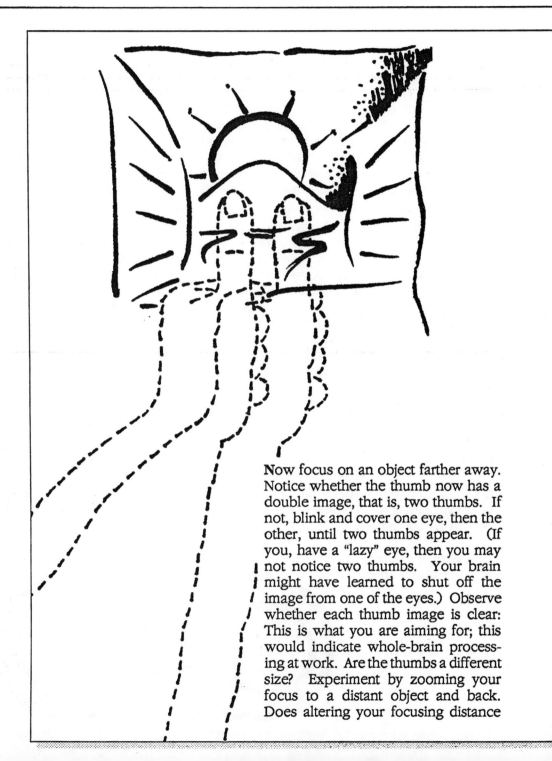

Now focus on an object farther away. Notice whether the thumb now has a double image, that is, two thumbs. If not, blink and cover one eye, then the other, until two thumbs appear. (If you, have a "lazy" eye, then you may not notice two thumbs. Your brain might have learned to shut off the image from one of the eyes.) Observe whether each thumb image is clear: This is what you are aiming for; this would indicate whole-brain processing at work. Are the thumbs a different size? Experiment by zooming your focus to a distant object and back. Does altering your focusing distance equality in size of the thumbs? What about wearing a patch over the eye that perceives the clearer thumb? Once again with your eyes open, are the thumbs a different size? What is the effect of breathing, standing, lying down, standing on one foot, on how you see the thumbs? Notice whether one thumb is higher than the other. What happens if you move your left ear toward your left shoulder? Does the higher thumb now look higher or lower? Yes, head posture will affect how well the input from each eye is accepted by the brain. If you read in bed or lie on your side, your two-eyed vision fitness will drop off. This means that your whole-brain processing will be less effective.

Once you've mastered maintaining an image of two relatively clear thumbs, pick up a book. Place your physical thumb halfway between the page and your eyes. Look at the printed page and while reading, move your physical thumb wherever your eyes go. Notice that when both eyes are being used (and two thumb images are perceived), you can see all of the words on the written page. Experiment by closing one eye. Observe that some of the words disappear because the remaining thumb blocks out part of your seeing. Let the thumb corresponding to the lesser perceiving channel lay over the words you're reading. Remember: if both eyes are working together, you will perceive two thumbs. If one of those thumbs goes away, blink, breathe, and look far away, and observe whether the disappearing thumb returns. Keep blinking, breathe, and palm your eyes.

If you become in too much of a "doing" state you will possibly notice one of the thumbs disappear, or the remaining thumb will cover the word(s) you're attempting to read. When this happens, there's a shift toward just left- or right-brain processing. This stressful imbalance is caused by one of the eye channel inputs not being accepted by the brain.

During your busy day, periodically let the thumb zapping vision fitness exercise verify your level of whole-brain seeing. Breathe, blink, and palm your eyes to remain whole-brain.

Circles Game:

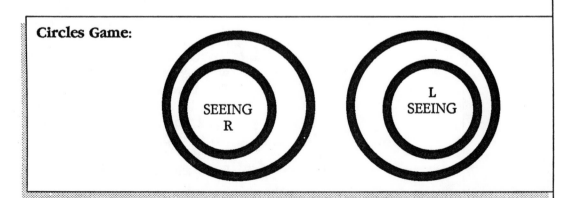

Recall what it feels like to cross your eyes. Hold up this book. Position the circles on page 68 at a distance of about 16 inches in front of your eyes. Cross your eyes ever so slightly, until there appear to be three circles. They may be quite blurry. Introduce breathing and crossing a little more or less. Does the blurriness increase or decrease? Repeat this process; perhaps zoom to far and then back until the middle picture appears clear. What do you see?

You may see the middle picture as follows:

1. An outer and inner circle
2. Also a word spelling SEEING
3. Or SEEING, but some of the letters disappear or run into each other
4. The word SEEING with an L on the top and an R on the bottom; they are in a straight line
5. The L and R move off center; they swim back and forth
6. The inner circle appears to float toward you

All these responses are possible. As your vision fitness fluctuates, so the way you perceive will change. An optimum two-eyed (whole-brain processing) level of vision fitness will result in a perfectly clear inner picture. You'll see a stable L and R and the word SEEING brightly. The letters will not move. You will be able to zoom to different distances, then re-aim your eyes and still see the three pictures.

Once you've mastered the eye-crossing phase, you'll be ready to do the exercise in the opposite way. This time look far away and introduce the target from a lowered position, below your line of vision. You might tend to want to look at the target; however, keep your attention focused far away. You'll discover a point where the three circles will appear. Answer the questions as before and explore the different phases your vision fitness and perception go through.

The importance of this vision fitness exercise is that you're teaching your eye-crossing muscles (centering) to work in partnership with the eye-focusing (ciliary) muscle. Usually when the eye-crossing muscles lack vision fitness, you'll automatically desire to over-focus, which can trigger development of nearsightedness or astigmatism.

How flexible is your vision fitness? Can you now form an image of three circles by crossing your eyes and then by looking far away? Alternate back and forth. Remember to incorporate breathing, blinking, yawning, and stretching your eye muscles. After five or 10 minutes of practicing, palm your eyes.

Mind's Eye:

The next best thing to a trampoline is a rebounder or mini-trampoline. If you have access to one of these bouncers, practice the exercises mentioned in Chapter 9 while jumping. You will be developing your mind's-eye seeing. Of course, you will ignore seat and knee drops. The mat is too small!

Arrow Game:

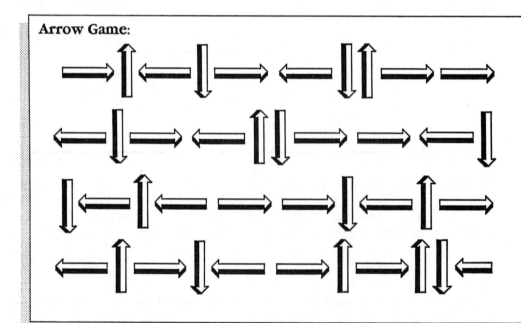

Make a large duplicate of the chart on page 70 and place it on a wall. Position yourself, without eyeglasses, at a distance where you can just make out the arrow directions. You'll be standing or sitting at what I call the "blur zone." For some of you this may be 10 inches or closer, while others may stand at 10 or 20 feet. Place equal weight on both feet if you're standing. Take three deep breaths.

STEP 1.   Begin at the top left corner and call out the direction of each arrow. Do you move your arms? Is your head still? Is your rhythm smooth? Are you aware of your breath? Do you try and see the arrow? Does your head or neck stretch forward?

NOTE: For each of the following steps, answer the above questions.

STEP 2.   Now call out and point the direction (using your arm) as well. Now do it backward from right to left.

STEP 3.   When pointing to the right, use your right hand. When pointing to the left, use your left hand. Right hand for up and left hand for down.

STEP 4.   Do the opposite of Step 3.

STEP 5.   In your mind's eye, imagine that the arrow has rotated 1/4 turn counterclockwise. Say that direction and don't point with your arms and hands. Observe whether there are any changes in your rhythm. Later, have a friend or family member clap their hands in rhythm; each time you hear the clap, call out the rotated direction. Observe how the clapping paces you. Do you maintain the same level of whole-brain processing or does a breakdown occur?

STEP 6.   Repeat Step 5, but now point your hands in the same direction you're saying.

STEP 7.   Repeat Step 5, but now point your hands in the direction that you see the arrow pointing. Record what feelings are present in your body. How do you respond? Do you get flustered, give up, or simply view the exercises as a challenge?

The arrow chart is particularly helpful for children and adults who have been told they have learning disabilities or are dyslexic. The whole-brain nature of the exercise teaches you how to handle overload. Mastery of each step probably stimulates more and more firing of different nerve connections in the brain. It's not uncommon for my patients to report a headachy feeling after such an exercise. I recall a teenager saying that it felt like the right side of her head was on fire after the arrow exercise. (If you should develop such sensations, palm your eyes and discontinue the exercise.)

The more you let go, or just be, the higher your level of whole-brain processing. Now is the chance to give up analyzing for a while. Trust your mind's eye and intuition. Let the exercise flow. Vision fitness exercises can be practiced whenever you have the desire to escape from your daily routine. Stay with the exercises for at least five minutes but no longer than one hour. The results will include improved work efficiency, greater clarity in communication, less eyestrain, improved sports ability, and less dependency on eyeglasses. Where else in your daily life can you transfer these feelings of "whole-brainedness"?

Enjoy your new vision!

PART FOUR

CLEARER VISION

12. IMPROVING YOUR EYESIGHT IN 21 DAYS

Introduction

The following 21-day vision improvement program was researched as a clinical study. (See Appendix for a summary of the research.) Its components are designed to work together synergistically when the entire program is practiced as outlined in this chapter.

However, let your individual needs and situation determine your level of involvement. You may wish to select or adapt specific exercises to meet a particular vision challenge. If so, I recommend that you flip back to the beginning of the book, and reread the material titled "How To Use This Book." Then read Chapter 12 once through, to familiarize yourself with all your options. The listing of "Vision Games For Your Specific Vision Challenges" may be especially helpful.

The 21-day total involvement program calls for a high degree of commitment. When first reading what there is to "do" each day, you might feel overwhelmed. The process is engrossing! Remember, however, that the purpose of the activities is to produce new, relaxed vision habits. There is an inherent risk that you will "TRY" and "DO" the program in an intense way— and fall into the "no pain, no gain" trap. *Seeing Beyond 20/20* is indeed based on a fitness model; however, aerobic and other fitness researchers are finding that brief non-strenuous activities are healthier than prolonged stress-inducing ones. Likewise, your eyes and mind's eye will prefer a relaxed involvement in the games. Then you can use your eye muscles and vision in a more natural and balanced way.

In fact, rather than thinking of each day's vision activity as an eye exercise, imagine it as a game. In this way you will be stimulating fun right-brain activity. This in turn will enhance whole-brain functioning.

The rationale for the three-week length of our program is that it takes approximately this period of time to imprint a new behavior or break an old habit. Your brain has been accustomed to one way of seeing the world. Now you will reeducate the brain in an orderly way, to enable new patterns of seeing to emerge.

The program is divided into 21 daily segments with activities and vision games for each day. The process is developmentally sequenced. Each day incorporates new levels of visual awareness and participation. Each of the three consecutive weeks will mark a transition to a more balanced mode of seeing.

One of the most important findings of my research studies was the value to my patients of support during the three weeks. Find someone who can support you. Ask this person to share your "highs" and "lows," to listen and encourage you when you are "down" and celebrate the "up" times. Your support person can be a counselor, eye doctor, friend, spouse, or therapist. Think of this person as your "buddy."

Again, doing more or trying harder is not necessarily better. Be awake, consistent, and aware. Choose a three-week period when you will have the time and be relaxed enough to implement the program.

Choose also your degree of participation, remembering that vision fitness develops when there is a balance between "doing" and "being." Focus on the activities that will promote relaxation, balance, and flow in your life. If you catch yourself worrying about things you haven't done, take a deep breath and modify your goals and the program. *Seeing Beyond 20/20* occurs with minimal effort.

Have fun, laugh, and play!

The 21-Day Activities

Before you undertake the 21-day adventure familiarize yourself with all of its components. The purpose of the program is to retrain vision fitness on as many levels as possible. For example:

❑ Setting goals will bring forth your "dream" into a vision and then tangible "sight."

❑ Using affirmations that personally address your vision and goals can bring your thinking and mind's-eye perceptions into alignment with your goals.

❑ Listening to a relaxation tape can alter and balance your brain wave patterns in order for you to use "whole-brain" perception. You can reprogram your thought patterns in the deepest "cells" of the brain.

❑ Eating better-balanced foods will alter the quality of the nutrients arriving at the eye. The different eye structures will receive therapeutic levels of vitamins and minerals.

❑ Excercising in an aerobic fashion or with quiet movements will reduce tension in the muscles and improve the blood flow.

❑ Spending time in natural light without eyeglasses or contacts will activate the part of the brain associated with natural light assimilation.

❑ Wearing the one-eyed patch will modify your perception through one of your eyes; wearing the two-eyed patch will create greater awareness of peripheral vision and enhanced clarity of sight without corrective lenses.

❑ Specific eye fitness games will increase your awareness of the eye structures, reduce tension and strain, and improve visual and overall body function.

❑ Recording your daily responses will give you feedback on your progress.

What follows is a more in-depth description of these program elements. Get a sense of what each part of the plan entails before you actually begin the program.

Some of the activities might be easy because you are aware of the process, while others might be more challenging. Be realistic when you set your goals. It is usually wiser to slowly build up your involvement in any one activity.

Setting Goals and Defining What You Wish to See!

When I think of goals I am reminded of the distinction between purpose and goal. Your purpose is long-term, like taking a journey to China. The goals of the trip will be to plan the finances, purchase the tickets, decide what to take, and read about the culture.

I view vision fitness in the same way. First, dream or have a "vision" about your ultimate purpose. Maybe it is giving up eyeglasses altogether or retaking your driver's test and passing without needing eyeglasses.

You may wish to improve your natural eyesight and still use weaker eyeglasses. Some of you might see new careers, reducing eyestrain, protecting your children's vision, or developing your physical fitness.

Each of these purposes has shorter measurable returns. I like to get the short-term goals in sight—see some outcome! Picture your purpose being associated with peripheral seeing (to do with the retina, and a future "vision"), and your goals—immediate specific results—with your foveal "sight" (what you can begin seeing now). Recall that foveal eyesight (looking) allows you to identify present aspects of your life. The retina (vision) permits observation of future or more peripheral aspects of your seeing. Everything you want to accomplish in life begins with defining a purpose and setting goals. Here is your chance to begin that process, for your vision and dreams (purpose) and for the more immediate goals of life.

At the beginning of the 21-day process, write down your long-term purpose and short-term goals for each of the sections. The career/work distinction is to assist those of you who may wish to make career changes. Relationships and money are included since many of my patients have made positive strides in these directions while they were improving their eyesight. I have provided a filled-out sample for you to get started.

* *Long Term*
** *Short Term*

YOUR PURPOSE AND GOALS

CAREER

* I see myself in a helping profession
* I wish to work with people in other countries
* I desire a service-oriented career
** Check out overseas work-study programs
** Call University about a Master's program

WORK

* Ultimately leave my current job of computer programming
* Be traveling, connected with people, and have sufficient income
** Contact the photographer to obtain part-time employment
** Prepare new resume outlining my photographic experience

RELATIONSHIPS

* Remarry
* Have one more child
** Continue to meet new friends
** Make two phone calls a week to acquaintances
** Make a list of how I view a partnership/relationship

MONEY

* Clear all my debts
* Have sufficient income to sustain my standard of living
** Obtain a new contract in next three weeks to clear car loan
** Structure the photographic work to provide X dollars for my living expenses
** Secure financial aid to go to school

EYES * Totally eliminate my dependency on eyeglasses
* Increase my vision fitness to a high enough degree that I can read
for three hours and maintain the same level of comprehension
* Heal the way the left eye works separately from the right eye
** Clear the redness in my eyes without eye drops
** Reduce my dependency on eyeglasses by 40 percent in three weeks
** Eliminate eyestrain associated with computer work by the
completion of the 21-day process

VISION

* To be traveling within two years
* Have a partnership/relationship in six months
* Improve my reading speed
* Incorporate relaxation into my daily life within two months
** Have photographs exhibited in two months
** "See" myself without eyeglasses in three weeks
** Visualize three new friends in one month

FOOD INTAKE * Become a total vegetarian
* Have my own organic vegetable garden
* Prepare foods according to the macrobiotic philosophy
** Eliminate red meat, turkey, and red fish for 21 days
** Eat no dairy products for one month
** Have fresh vegetables at every meal for three weeks
** Eliminate all Alcohol and tobacco during the 21 day program

BODY EXERCISE

* Run a marathon
* Exercise every day
* Reduce my waistline and increase upper-body muscle strength
** Jog on a trampoline every other day
** Walk two miles three times a week
** Ride five miles on a bicycle twice a week

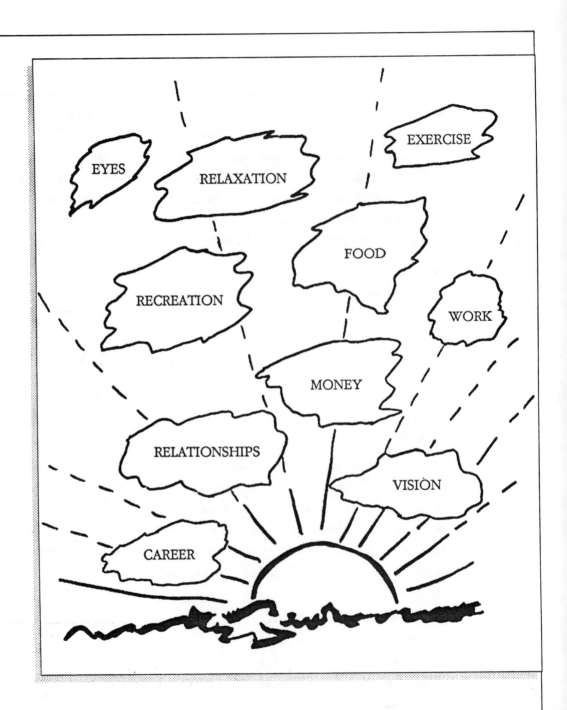

Your Purpose and Goals

CAREER

_____

_____

_____

_____

_____

_____

WORK

_____

_____

_____

_____

_____

_____

RELATIONSHIPS

_____

_____

_____

_____

_____

_____

MONEY

_____

_____

_____

_____

_____

EYES

VISION

FOOD INTAKE

BODY EXERCISE

Affirmations

One way to modify your thinking, and the way your mind's eye perceives, is to make use of affirmations. These are positive statements that are usually stated aloud or written. At first you might find the exercise silly or even disbelieve its value. The goal is to repeat saying an affirmation until there is an inner shift from negative thinking to positive.

Think of an affirmation as adding new software for the hardware (your brain or mind). In response to the affirmation, your conscious mind might first say: "No!" or "It's blurry—I can't see!" Yet the new software will be recorded on the "silicon chip" of the unconscious. The new data will later register at the conscious level.

For example: A patient with 20/80 eyesight or 58.5 percent vision fitness may affirm: "I will pass my driver's test in one month." The patient's first inner response might be: "No way!" After a few times the response might be: "Well, it's possible!" Later still the feeling is: "Yes! I am going for it." The brain/mind's-eye relationship has shifted. Now the possibility exists for the patient to reach her goal.

Stand in front of the Eye-C chart while saying the affirmations. Record the visual responses to the affirmations as + (improvement), neutral (no change), and - (decreased sight). The affirmations that have a positive effect on your seeing are already coded "positively" in the brain "cells." These affirmations can be used to further enhance your vision when you experience the natural blur, or blur through your vision fitness lenses, becoming more intense. Also keep using the affirmations that produce neutral or negative results. Perhaps your unconscious is resisting the intended message of these affirmations. Incorporating them into the 21-day program will modify your unconscious perception of the affirmation into a positive feeling.

Here are some affirmations that you can use during the 21 days. Whether you choose from among these or make up your own, use affirmations that personally address your vision and goals. State the affirmation throughout the day, perhaps while you play the vision games, wear patches, exercise, or prepare meals.

My vision is improving every day

I am reducing my dependency on eyeglasses in every way

My sight is improving

I am in touch with why I block my perception

I enjoy the way I see

I love my blur

I am embracing my blur each day

I am having fun exploring my blur

I look forward to seeing less blur

I am enjoying the way I look and see

Vision is my creating the way I see

I now see the truth

I see the beauty of life

I forgive my parents' perceptions

I see the truth of my early environment

When I see the truth of my upbringing, I feel free

It is now OK for my eyes to see

I am focusing my perception on my visions

I am conscious of my state of being aiding my vision

I am in touch with what I see in my blur

I like the softness in the way I see

My mind's eye guides my outer sight

I am powerful and I am healing my eyes

I feel less vulnerable without my eyeglasses

I have clear and healthy vision

I am experiencing clear flashes of sight

I love life; therefore my vision of life is clear

It is safe for me to see

I forgive myself and my vision is now clear

My negative patterns of seeing are now dissolving

My vision is perfect as I observe my perfection

I nourish myself with healthy foods and exercise

I love my body, my eyes, and vision

It is easy for me to recover my vision

I now deal with tension that blurs my vision

I am removing the obstructions to seeing the beauty of the world

I see the wisdom and truth in life

I am in touch with the inner desire to see

I am working through the barriers of ignorance, fear, and anger so that my perfect vision is being realized

I am thankful that my vision is healthy and clear

I see things in the world that please me

My glasses are now becoming less a part of me

I am letting healthy, alive, and creative vision manifest itself

I am projecting my new consciousness through my eyes

My evening vision is as clear as my daytime vision

I see more colors with my natural vision

As I enjoy my body, my vision becomes clearer

As my mind becomes clear and balanced, I see more

I am magnificent; I am empowering myself and others with love, light, and vision

Relaxation

An integral part of the 21-day program is to train your mind and body how to relax via suggestions. Trained patients have been able to induce relaxation by talking to body parts and eyes.

The eyes, especially, will quickly learn to relax. In the beginning, as in any new training program, you will slowly introduce specific suggestions.

One way to accomplish this is to listen to relaxing music. The choice of music could span quiet jazz, baroque, classical, or the modern "New Age" piano, flute, harp, and electronic keyboard varieties. The key is to "unwind" the mind, which in turn relaxes the body and many of the physiological processes, like the heartbeat and breathing.

Ultimately the eyes and the process of vision will be facilitated by this relaxation. The goal is to reach the point where you can, at will, induce a relaxed state during stressful periods of the day.

While researching *Seeing Beyond 20/20*, I wrote a narrative that was later turned into a "Relax and See" audio tape. To simulate the male/female association for the right and left eyes respectively, I made use of two voices. My voice leads the listener on a relaxing journey, while an audible female voice states visually related affirmations.

Measured during clinical testing, the effects were very dramatic. Most of the subjects were unable to complete the 26-minute tape because they inevitably fell asleep. The average falling asleep time seemed to be 12 minutes after the tape began. They also reported a profound overall feeling of body, mind, and eye relaxation as well as dreaming in vivid pictures.

From this it appears that the unconscious mind is still recording the suggestions from the tape while the listener enters initial stages of sleep. It is the repetitious listening to the taped suggestions for three weeks that creates the habit of relaxing.

More recently, I have been producing custom-made audio tapes* for my patients, based on their answers to an in-depth questionnaire.

*If you would like to acquire this or other tapes, see "Products For Seeing Beyond 20/20," page 163.

The results have been most encouraging:

> "Your voice is extraordinary... my eyes are measurably stronger. I now see twice as far and no longer squint... I look forward to my next reduced lens prescription."
>
> "The tape has brought fast results... my left eye is no longer blurry and tired... I can read again without strain."

Of course, the benefits of feeding suggestions to the unconscious mind don't have to stop at relaxation. Prior to sleeping I use tapes or imagine specific statements in my unconscious mind.

Such a statement may be a form of acknowledgment, a thought to dream about, or an answer I seek to a specific challenge in my life.

Eating

You're going to be asking a lot from your eyes over the next 21 days, so you'll want to nourish them with foods that will contribute to your natural vision fitness. Set up an eating plan, and stick to it! (For some helpful guidelines, refer back to Chapter Six, "Nutrition And Aerobics For Your Eyes.")

In case you slip and succumb to a "forbidden" food (and even if you don't slip at all), use the biofeedback nature of your eyes to monitor how various foods affect your vision fitness. With every food you eat, you can experiment to learn more about your own body's needs.

If you would like to replicate what the research subjects omitted and included in their eating program for the 21 days, use the following summary.

Foods and substances that patients refrained from eating for the 21 days included:

Alcoholic beverages	Eggs
Caffeinated foods and drinks	Fried foods
Caffeinated tea	Fruit
Canned food	Fruit juices
Cheese	Ice cream
Cigarettes	Milk
Coffee	Red meat
Drugs (unless under medical direction)	Sugared items

Preferred foods for the 21 days include:

One salad per day

Raw/steamed/lightly cooked vegetables every day

Herb (chamomile) or bancha (twig) tea

Fasting for one day (speak to your physician) (Fasting can involve drinking only water or drinking vegetable or fruit juices)

Seasoning as recommended in macrobiotic cookbooks (see Bibliography)

One serving of fish or poultry every other day instead of red meat (if vegetarian, use bean derivatives)

Tofu (bean curd)/mochi (sweet rice)/tempeh (from soybean)

Grains such as short-grain brown rice, millet, quinoi (Incan grain), kasha (buckwheat groats), basmati rice (long-grain Indian variety)

Root vegetables and squashes

Natural multivitamin/mineral supplement (See "Products For Seeing Beyond 20/20")

Body Exercise

As you may recall from Chapter Six, exercising your body will increase the efficiency with which the blood can circulate nutrients to your eyes.

I have my patients select one or more movement or exercise activities to use during the 21 days. Here are some suggestions:

Aerobics	Skiing
Backpacking	Slow dancing
Cycling	Swimming
Exercise bike	Tai chi
Fast dancing	Tennis
Jogging	Walking
Raquetball	Weights
Rowing	Wind surfing
Skating	Yoga

Natural Light

Most books on the anatomy of the eye mention how 25 percent of the visual fibers that leave the retina bypass the pathways to the visual area of the brain. It has been proposed that these fibers, carrying the electrical equivalent of white sunlight, go to a part of the brain known as the hypothalamus. This "master regulator" makes adjustments to the nervous system of the body, balancing the functions of organs like the pituitary and adrenal glands. Also, a pea-size organ known as the pineal gland, thought to be the primitive eye, or our "third eye," is apparently "charged" by the full-spectrum white light traversing the hypothalamus. This charge may also have some influence on the balance in the nervous system. This could possibly affect mood states or accuracy of our perceptions.

Thus it appears that the natural full-spectrum white sunlight keeps the bodily functions working at a minimal physiological level. In the absence of full-spectrum light, the autonomic nervous system has to make an internal adjustment. This adjustment can manifest as fatigue, a desire to eat "culprit foods," irritability, and mood shifts. This is why it is necessary for you to spend periods of time (20 to 30 minutes per day) out of doors without eye devices that block natural sunlight, including sunglasses or prescription eyeglasses, or contacts.

If the weather is pleasant, practice the vision games outside as well. Remember to not look directly at the sun or have any harsh sunlight reflecting off reading material. Staring at the sun could cause damage to the fovea, while unnecessary reflections can contribute to eyestrain.

Patches

There are two kinds of patches you will be using during the 21 days.

Week 1/One-Eyed Patch

For Week 1 you will cover your preferred eye (the eye you would sight with if you were looking down a telescope). If you wish to wear your eyeglasses you may place a piece of paper behind one of the lenses to act as a patch (see also "Products For Seeing Beyond 20/20").

The optimum patching time would be for four continuous hours per day. In the beginning you might find it helpful to set up a wearing schedule that gradually increases. For the first day you could wear the patch for one hour; then on Day 2, two hours, etc. Decide what works for you according to your schedule and unique level of vision fitness.

The four-hour patch-wearing stretch may include activities like cooking, physical exercise (but in a safe environment—and never while driving!), watching TV, doing laundry, reading, working at a desk or on a computer, taking a walk in a park, talking with friends, etc. You could also include the time you are playing the visual games as part of the four hours (see description of individual games for any specific instructions on patch-wearing).

The one-eyed patch will stimulate perceptions and memories. You might have physical or even emotional responses. Record these experiences on your Clearer Vision Daily Goals Sheet. If you are covering the right eye, observe whether or not your speech patterns change. If your left eye is covered, notice whether it is more difficult to hear or listen to what others are saying. Connect the right/left brain aspects of *Seeing Beyond 20/20.* While wearing the patch you might notice your speed at "getting things done" to be slower. You will be learning how to negotiate the blur. This is a very important part of the training process. Many of my patients are thankful to slow down and "see" more of life.

Remove the patch very slowly at first. What happens when you remove the patch after an extended wearing period? Does your physical or emotional balance change? Enjoy the light when the patch comes off.

By the way, I encourage my patients to place stickers on their patches. In this way, if they go "public," then others will want to know what is going on! While working on my own vision, and by going public, I learned a lot when I shared with others. Of course, you can choose to be in the "closet."

Week 2/Two-Eyed Patch

During Week 2, you will put aside the one-eyed patch, and wear instead a two-eyed patch. This new patch is designed to create in you the awareness of peripheral (seeing as opposed to looking) vision, and to foster greater clarity of sight without corrective lenses.

To make the two-eyed patch, cut out a 3 inch by 1 inch strip of stiff cardboard (like a visiting card). Remove a triangular piece to accommodate your nose.

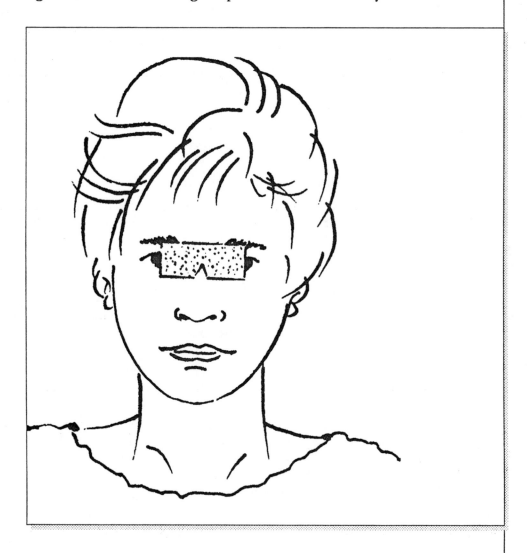

Wear your two-eyed patch instead of corrective lenses for four consecutive hours a day during Week 2. (It bears repeating: wear your patch in non-life-threatening situations only.) Once again, the wearing period can include your game-playing time; refer to each day's game instructions for any specific guidelines on patch-wearing. In addition to this week's new games, you will be repeating Week 1 games while wearing the two-eyed patch.

Be sure to experiment with the new patch. Rotate your head to the left or right, and notice whether you perceive more easily or clearly through one side. Does this correspond to your preferred eye? Now, move your head so that you perceive more out of the other, non-preferred eye, to develop its vision fitness. Observe how you feel while wearing the two-eyed patch. Do you tend to relax more, or less? Whatever you feel while wearing the patch, see if you can recreate that sensation when not wearing the patch.

As before, don't hesitate to decorate your patch and venture with it into public places. Be brave! People will be genuinely interested in hearing about your program, and you might make some new friends.

Week 3/Either Patch Worn Outside Of Games

Throughout Week 3 you will not be wearing any patch while playing vision games, so that you can strengthen the ability of your eyes to work together . But continue to wear either the one-eyed or the two-eyed patch every day for four continuous hours.

Vision Games

The vision fitness exercises, or what I will call vision games, are distributed over the three-week period. I like to describe the vision work as a game so that you have fun incorporating the "play" into your daily life.

There is a new game for each day. Each vision game calls for a higher degree of vision fitness as you move through the 21 days (see Summary Of The Vision Games, page 103).

If you decide not to do the 21-day program in its entirety, the vision games can be practiced out of sequence. For example, if you find a game that is particularly effective for your needs, play with it and develop your vision fitness. If you find the game too complex, go back to an earlier day's vision game and master that activity before proceeding to a higher level.

When working on Day 2, you will repeat Day 1's game and so on. This means that when you are on Day 11, you'll play the game for Day 11, and repeat all the games for the first 10 days. You will be working toward mastery of each activity and developing your vision fitness in a systematic and developmental way.

Once you have completed Week 1, then you will repeat Week 1 games with the two-eyed patch and also begin Week 2 games. Both eyes will have a chance to increase their vision fitness playing the one-eyed games while wearing the two-eyed patch.

In the third week, you repeat Week 1 and Week 2 games with both eyes open. This week you will be training the cells in the brain that respond to two-eyed activity; hence the reason for discarding the patch during the games. Don't forget to still wear either the one-eyed patch or two-eyed patch for four continuous hours daily during Week 3.

Some suggestions: Remember to remove your contacts and/or eyeglasses during the vision games. In some cases you might experiment using your reduced lens prescription. Read the activity for each day, and re-read it when you play the vision game. Also, set aside a specific time for your vision games on your Clearer Vision Daily Goals Sheet, recognizing that Weeks 2 and 3 will require more time to play.

Notice that I make specific mention of those vision games that are helpful for dyslexia; reading problems; eye "dis-ease," computer work and other causes of eyestrain; farsightedness; nearsightedness; and astigmatism. Rather than becoming involved in the whole program, many patients choose individual games from throughout the program that can help them overcome particular vision challenges. The following summary indicates games that are helpful for training vision fitness in specific instances.

Vision Games for Your Specific Vision Challenges

Farsightedness	Zooming, Near Eye-C chart, Lighting, Fencing
Nearsightedness	Far Eye-C chart, Soft Focus, Imaging, Painting
Astigmatism	Painting, Palming, Eye Muscle Stretch, Fencing
Eye "Dis-ease"	Imaging, Acupressure, Yawning, Palming
Computer-Related & Other Eyestrain	Zooming, Eye-C chart, Shifting, Palming
Dyslexia	Marching, Swing Ball, String Thing, Fencing
Slow Reading	String Thing, Fencing, Finger Doubling, Circles
Children's Vision	Palming, Swing Ball, Fencing, Lighting, Eye Muscle Stretch, Marching

With children I have them play any of these vision games whenever the commercials come on during their television watching.

Record Keeping

Review your overall goals at the transition point from one week to the next. Each day complete the "Results Produced" sheet, filling in results, Eye-C chart measurements and the Physical and Emotional Responses section of the sheet. Also fill in the "Clearer Vision Daily Goals" form for the next day, choosing the affirmation and goals for the day, and the times you plan to implement the goals. By the time you complete the 21 days you should have a complete diary of your adventures. Here is a sample filled-in sheet for you to use as a guide.

Clearer Vision Daily Goals

WEEK _One_ DAY _Four_

AFFIRMATION _I am enjoying how I see myself and the world_

GOALS IMPLEMENTATION TIME

GOAL #

	GOALS	Goal #	Time	Goal #	Time
1	Wear one-eyed patch	1	7am	9	5pm
2	Do vision games	1	8am	6	6pm
3	Jump on rebounder	1; 7	9am	4	7pm
4	Prepare healthy meal	1; 2	10am		8pm
5	Listen to relaxation tape	1	11am	10	9pm
6	Call Lucy for support	4	12noon		10pm
7	Complete work on computer		1pm	5	11pm
8	Prepare budget for Joe	3	2pm		
9	Work on resume	8	3pm		
10	Meditate		4pm		

NOTES: Tomorrow, remember to update record keeping
Make note to call new friend
Use vision games on the computer
Record how long I go without eyeglasses tomorrow
Have Susan photograph my eye so I can track the redness
Call the gallery to see if they will exhibit photo

RESULTS PRODUCED

1 Able to wear the patch for three hours today
2 The vision games really relax my eyes
3 Had a clear flash today - 30 percent gain
4 I am beginning to believe the affirmation
5 The food tasted great tonight
6 Tried using the patch while on the trampoline
7 I am realizing that leaving my job is a reality

	FAR		NEAR
EYE-C Chart	RIGHT	50 at 5 feet	20 at 16 inches
	LEFT	60 at 5 feet	20 at 16 inches
	BOTH	40 at 5 feet	20 at 16 inches

PHYSICAL AND EMOTIONAL RESPONSES:

The patch produced a weird sensation of falling
Jumping on the trampoline with the patch
required a major readjustment
After the second hour of wearing the patch over
my left eye, I felt some anger towards my father
The clear flash of sight made me feel sad
I am feeling very confident about this program

Clearer Vision Daily Goals

WEEK _____ DAY _____

AFFIRMATION _____

_____

GOALS   IMPLEMENTATION TIME

                                             GOAL #

1 _____   _____ 7am   _____ 5pm

2 _____   _____ 8am   _____ 6pm

3 _____   _____ 9am   _____ 7pm

4 _____   _____ 10am _____ 8pm

5 _____   _____ 11am _____ 9pm

6 _____   _____ 12noon _____ 10pm

7 _____   _____ 1pm   _____ 11pm

8 _____   _____ 2pm

9 _____   _____ 3pm

10 _____   _____ 4pm

NOTES: _____

_____

_____

_____

_____

RESULTS PRODUCED

1 _____
2 _____
3 _____
4 _____
5 _____
6 _____
7 _____

		FAR		NEAR
EYE-C Chart	RIGHT	_____		_____
	LEFT	_____		_____
	BOTH	_____		_____

PHYSICAL AND EMOTIONAL RESPONSES:

_____
_____
_____
_____
_____
_____
_____
_____
_____
_____
_____
_____
_____

Summary of Vision Games for the 21 Days

	DAY	GAME FOR THE DAY
WEEK 1		
ONE-EYED PATCH	1	ZOOMING
	2	PALMING
	3	EYE-C CHART
	4	SOFT FOCUS
	5	PAINTING/YAWNING
	6	SWING BALL
	7	SHIFTING/SCANNING
WEEK 2		
TWO-EYED PATCH		
	8	NOSE PENCIL
	9	LIGHTING
	10	DYNAMIC VISUAL MEDITATION
	11	EYE MUSCLE STRETCH
	12	MARCHING
	13	ACUPRESSURE
	14	SHOULDER AND NECK MASSAGE
WEEK 3		
NO PATCH		
	15	STRING THING
	16	FENCING
	17	THUMB ZAPPING
	18	FINGER DOUBLING
	19	CIRCLES
	20	IMAGING
	21	MAINTENANCE PROGRAM

Week 1 (Note: Wear the one-eyed patch)

Day 1 Zooming

Purpose   To train flexible focus between your mind and physical eyes.

Materials   Your thumb, an eraser, a window, a person's face, or any nearby object that is at a distance between your eyes and farther objects at which you are looking.

Instructions Zooming means to change focus from a near distance to a far distance. For instance, imagine looking from a nearby red flower to a distant forest.

Sit comfortably in a chair and position your thumb or index finger in front of your non-patched eye.

Take a deep breath in from three inches below the navel, and imagine air flowing into your eyes. (This is the type of breathing you can use with all the vision games.)

While looking at your finger, become aware of how blurry everything is beyond the finger. "See" to the right, left, up, and down while you continue looking at the finger.

The more you can be aware of the blur, the clearer the thumb will appear. This awareness of blur around the point you are looking at is helpful for improving fitness of your foveal eyesight. Let the blur represent your awareness of your retina.

Now move your focus of attention toward an object farther from your eyes. Repeat to farther and farther distances. Repeat changing your focus back and forth from the near to distant object.

Now walk around the room you're in seeing everything, while either looking at your finger or a distant point.

Look at the blur as a connection to your past vision. See beyond your limiting filters of the past; dissolve the memory implant that says you can't see. As you zoom back and forth, experience your vision now free of the belief filters of the past. Imagine that your brain and eyes have the internal knowing of how to produce self-healing.

Zoom and see now as an observer with little or no thinking. Feel what you see rather than think. Zooming allows you to move out into your visual world through the blur.

Repeat the zooming for 10 to 20 breaths three times during the day.

Observations Catch yourself staring, holding your breath, or not blinking.

Do you have any physical reactions like tension spots in the stomach, shoulders, neck, or behind the head?

How safe do you feel as you reach out into the blur?

Do you experience any feelings of sadness, happiness, joy, terror, nervousness, loneliness, or anxiety? Do you feel an urge to rip off the patch?

Week 1

Day 2 Palming

Purpose   To use your healing hands to direct specific energy and images to and from the eyes.

Instructions   Make yourself comfortable by resting your elbows on a table or placing a pillow on your chest to rest your arms.

Gently rub your palms together, generating warmth.

Place your warm palms over your relaxed, closed eyelids. The palms should not be pressed against the eyes but should gently rest on the bony ridge surrounding the eyes.

Imagine that your palms are like magnets that can draw out tension from the eyelids, the inside and outside muscles.

During the colder months imagine the warmth being like a down comforter or a sleeping bag that is warming the structures of the eye.

Visualize the different parts of the eyes relaxing the way your body muscles let go in a hot bath.

Feel the warmth from your palms as you breathe.

Imagine, with each breath, healthy blood flowing from the heart, up the spine, into your brain, down the optic nerve, and into the eye.

Picture the healthy blood carrying oxygen for the tears and all the nutrients from the healthy foods you are eating. Let the vitamins and minerals flow to the eye structures: Vitamin A and zinc to the retina; B-complex to the macula and fovea; chromium to the focusing muscle; and vitamins C, E and B_2 to the lens, which remolds to a perfect shape for 20/20 vision.

Palm for a minimum of two minutes, twice or three times per day. You could palm for as long as 15 minutes and use this as your daily relaxation exercise.

Observations While palming, can you produce a color sensation of deep blue or violet?   Is there a relationship between thinking and not seeing the dark color?

Does your mind or inner voice interfere with this vision game?

Can you slow down your breathing?

How do you feel about your blur when removing your palms?

Do you notice how bright everything appears?

Do objects appear clearer?

When your eyes open, can you pretend you have full use of your vision?

Be ready to have clear flashes of perfect sight!

Reminder Remember to repeat the vision game from Day 1!

Week 1

Day 3   Eye-C Chart

Purpose   To observe and become aware of how relaxation, mind strain, affirmations, foods, stress, and light affect your perceptions on a simulated eye chart.

Materials   There are two Eye-C charts.   The bigger Distance Eye-C chart is used at a distance of five feet. Have a copy made of the chart at the end of the book or remove the chart itself.   Place the Distance Eye-C chart on a wall five feet away. The smaller Near Eye-C chart is held at approximately 16 inches.

Instructions   If your challenge is blur in the distance, then start out using the Distance Eye-C chart. If things up close are blurry, then use the Near Eye-C chart.

Distance   Have enough light shining on the chart. Use a 100-watt daylight blue color-corrected light bulb (see Products For Seeing Beyond 20/20) shining from a three-foot distance.

Stand or sit at your chosen distance of 5, 10, 15, or 20 feet. Choose a distance at which you can just make out the letters in the middle of the chart. Make sure you have patched your preferred eye and see which letters on the Eye-C chart are clear enough for you to make out.

This is not a test. You are training yourself to be relaxed in front of a simulated eye chart. This awareness will result in you being more comfortable and skilled when going back to your eye doctor to have your eyes and vision measured. If you can train yourself to be very comfortable, confident, and relaxed with the Eye-C chart, the regular Snellen chart will be easier to perceive. Your eye doctor's measurements will then be made under more relaxed conditions.

Make a note on your Clearer Vision Daily Goals Sheet of which line you can see. Record the vision fitness number alongside the line as well as the distance from your eyes to the chart. If you like you can also verify how the patched eye is perceiving.

Some patients make clear transparencies of the Distance Eye-C chart and place them on windows. In that way you can look through the chart while still maintaining your seeing of the chart. (This will be covered in more detail on Days 15 through 19.)

Later on in the three weeks you will learn more advanced looking and seeing strategies that can be practiced while playing the Eye-C chart game.

Near   Have a good light source (100-watt bulb shining on the chart from a distance of three feet).

Hold the chart at a distance equivalent to the distance from your middle knuckle to your elbow or whatever distance allows you to clearly see some of the letters.

Have your preferred eye covered with the patch. If you cannot make out any letters or words, then slip on your reduced reading lens prescription.

The goal of the game is to be able to make out smaller and smaller print, letters, or words. Note the vision fitness number on the line of print that you can make out on the Eye-C chart. Move the chart back and forth and see if through relaxation you can keep the letters clear as you bring the chart closer to your eyes. Spend about five minutes playing with the Eye-C chart.

Make extra copies to place in different parts of your home or office. As you walk by the Eye-C chart, glance and check your ability to perceive. In this way you can begin using your eyes as the biofeedback device I spoke about in Chapter Three. When there is a great variation, begin looking for what is causing the change.

Observations While playing with the Eye-C charts, begin incorporating earlier games like zooming, palming, breathing, and blinking.

Zoom from the Distance Eye-C chart to the near one and vice versa.

If you are using the distance chart, zoom onto your index finger or thumb at six inches from your eyes. Breathe in when you look up close and out when you zoom far away. How does it feel when you breathe? Do you observe clear flashes of the letters?

Imagine white light emanating from the Eye-C charts as opposed to letters. Absorb and receive this white light with no expectation about the clarity of the letters.

The idea is to let go of trying to make the letters clear. The clear flashes will happen on their own; you do not have to try and make this happen. Actually, trying defeats the purpose of clearer vision. Trying "harder" is a cultural bad habit that many of us have imprinted into our belief system.

Week 1

Day 4 Soft Focus

Purpose   To train yourself to be able to look in a relaxed way while seeing.

Materials   Use the Distance or Near Eye-C charts or any other object that has details.

Instructions As in zooming, become aware of the object or detail you are looking at. Let the point of focus (object) represent your fovea in space. Let the area around the looking point (background) be the retina in space. As long as you are looking and seeing simultaneously, you will be simulating a soft focus.

Unlike my earlier suggestions, soft focus can be done for short (five to 25 seconds) periods of non-blinking. Usually a lack of blinking implies that you're staring. By following the above directions no harm will result by delaying your blinking. I have seen patients go without blinking for 60 seconds and longer while soft focusing. Observe whether or not blinking pulls your vision closer toward the clearer zone of seeing.

Systematic diaphragm breathing is the important variable. As long as the breath is flowing, you will be in soft focus rather than staring.

Soft focus can be played while you read, work on the computer terminal, and play sports.

If you are wearing your regular strong eyeglasses you can use soft focus to prevent staring. While soft focusing, imagine you are moving out into your visual world, as if you are looking through the blur.

Soft focus for five minutes per day.

Observations In the beginning, catch yourself when you are not soft focusing. Then move into soft focusing.

Can you soft focus at work, while cooking, cleaning house, going for a walk, or watching TV?

Do you feel more balanced when you soft focus? Begin soft focusing on the parts of yourself you may not have wished to see. These may have to do with hidden talents; desire for a new job or different relationship, or friends/family that you have neglected.

Week 1

Day 5 Painting/Yawning

Purpose To teach the mind's eye to see white, to release tension in the jaw and face muscles, and produce flowing tears so as to bathe the cornea.

Instructions Begin with yawning. Granted, it is considered bad manners in our culture to yawn. However, for this game you can imagine permission has been granted for you to yawn.

I am talking about a loud animal yawn where the jaws are wide open and you expel sounds through your mouth. To release your inhibitions, imagine that you are visiting the zoo and you are playing with the chimpanzees. Let go of all the holds you have on expressing animal sounds. Let others around you know about the game you are playing.

Play the yawning game until the tears flow down your cheeks. When you produce tears, imagine that the toxins within the eyes are flowing away and healthy nutrients are flowing in.

After a while you might find the yawning game quite relaxing, and the clear flashes will increase in frequency.

Now that you feel relaxed and more present, close your eyes.

Imagine a paintbrush placed on the end of your nose. By moving your head you can paint anything you wish with the brush.

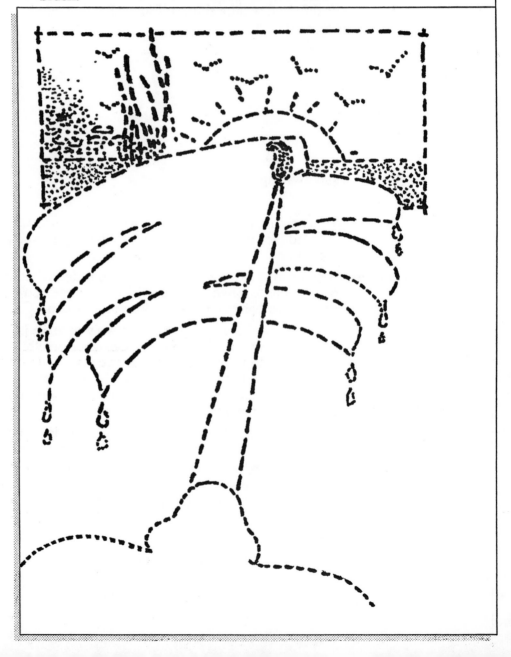

In the beginning, imagine the only paint you have is white, and as a game, you are going to paint everything in sight white. You can begin with your bedroom, then the living room, the rest of your home, your place of work. Enjoy seeing everything white in your mind's eye.

Painting teaches you to enjoy white, the light emitted by the sun with all the colors present. This game is also designed to familiarize you with the idea of being able to see white. As you will experience in Week 2, white light can be used for self-healing. Paint the Eye-C chart so that all the letters are covered. Experience in your mind's-eye seeing the white light beaming off the chart and coming into your eyes and your third eye (between your eyes on your forehead).

Give a few more yawns to help see the whiteness. Spend five to 10 minutes playing these two games.

Observations Find other times during the day when you could yawn or paint. If you travel on a bus or by train, close your eyes and image the persons around you, and paint them white. When you are driving and are waiting at stoplights, give a mighty yawn. Grade yourself on the intensity of the yawns.

Sit in front of the Eye-C chart. After a yawning spell and two or three minutes spent painting white, observe the letters on the chart. Are you able to see more, or less, clearly? Are you able to relax your mind—that is, your thinking—during this vision game?

Talk to your brain and let it know that you would like to see more clearly in three weeks!

Week 1

Day 6 Swing Ball

Purpose   To activate and integrate all the parts of the brain into synchronous whole-brain perceptions.

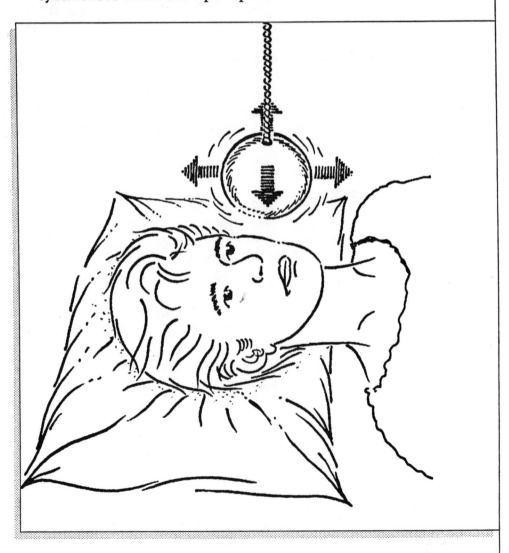

Materials Obtain a soft colored ball about three inches in diameter. Attach a 10-foot string to the ball by bending a large paper clip and pushing it through the ball.

Attach the string to a plant hook from the ceiling. Adjust string length so that when you are lying down underneath the ball it will be about 16 inches from your eyes.

Reminder Remember to use the one-eyed patch during Week 1, the two-eyed patch during Week 2, and no patch during Week 3.

Instructions Lie underneath the ball on a comfortable surface like a carpet, mat, or bed. Make sure that your entire body is relaxed.

Let the ball be directly in front of your uncovered eye or eyes. Look at the ball and see all the other areas of space around the ball. Let your vision wander around the room while you look at the ball. (Remember, your fovea is represented by the ball and the retina is the rest of the space.)

Follow the same directions as in Zooming and the other vision games you have been mastering. Breathe as you zoom from the ball to the ceiling. Imagine more and more areas of space coming into focus.

This phase of Swing Ball is mastered without the influence of gravity. Later you will repeat the same game, while standing.

Some of my patients have been creative, placing an Eye-C chart on the ceiling where the string is attached. Try this. You can then observe changes in visual clarity as you play the swing ball game.

Touch the ball so that it begins swinging from above your head toward your feet. Use Baroque music to create rhythm during the game. I have found Vivaldi's *Four Seasons* a good choice.

Tune in to your breathing as you train your eyes to follow the swinging ball. The goal is to keep your mind and eyes free of strain.

Become aware of how space, other than the ball, seems to be moving by really fast. This is like being on a fast-moving train, looking out the window watching the nearby scenery zooming by.

You might feel squeezing or warm sensations in the stomach or chest area. Repeat this phase until your body and mind feel more relaxed.

Patients have learned to feel their bodies and emotions more during the swing ball game. It would seem that the up and down motion of the ball might affect the seven energy centers of the body. These centers are also known as chakras. It is possible that as you follow the ball, the motion of your eyes directs a flow of energy to the center corresponding to the position of the ball. For example, when the ball is positioned over the heart area, the eyes are looking in that direction. It is therefore possible that the energy center associated with the heart chakra is then stimulated. My personal experience is that I feel more connection between my body, mind, spirit, and eyes after five minutes of this phase of swing ball.

For the next phase, follow the ball as it swings left and right across your uncovered eye(s), maintaining the same 16-inch distance. Now the left and right movement of your eyes will be synchronizing the different brain hemispheres. Research has shown that when the eyes look to the left, you are stimulating the right hemisphere, and vice versa. Crossing over at the midline of the eyes leads to a very powerful "switching" that helps in the integration process within the brain.

Many patients with motion sickness have been helped by this exercise alone. I remember a dyslexic patient at this point in the game saying: "I think my eye is drunk!"

Repeat for 20 to 50 breaths. You should feel your eyes moving very smoothly during the left to right movement. Let the swing ball set the rhythm for your breathing.

Every now and again, zoom to the ceiling and then come back to the ball. How quickly can you change focus?

When you have mastery, add another variable. This time when the ball goes to the right say "right," and when the ball goes to the left say "left." Repeat until you feel total flow, and trust that you can effortlessly play the game.

Now say the opposite. Call out "left" when the ball swings to the right and "right" when the ball swings to the left. Say it aloud!

Then, lift your left arm up when your eyes go to the left and you say "right" and vice versa.

As you can see, the game can become quite complex and require a lot of memory, trust, and vision.

What you can remember, you can see!

When you are ready for another challenge, choose a word to spell. When the ball goes to the left, without moving your arms, spell the first letter. Spell the second letter when the ball goes to the right.

Pay attention to the movement of your eyes rather than your head. I notice that when patients begin thinking about the word, as opposed to picturing, the eyes tend to stop moving.

When your vision fitness at this level is developed, include arm and even leg movements with the spelling.

Lastly, choose two words. Spell one of the words on the right side while the other word is spelled on the left side. If the two words were Texas and Oregon, you would start off by designating Texas to the left and Oregon to the right. When the ball swings to the right, you spell O, then follow the ball to the left and spell T, and so you continue. This calls for high degrees of visual imagery, memory, sequencing, and visual attention.

You can later introduce right arm and left leg movements while you spell in this way. Again, relaxing music can be used, or you can move to the stage where you add rock music to act as a distractor.

The goal is to be able to play the swing ball game while spelling, moving the assigned body parts, and listening to potentially distracting music. Then repeat the whole process standing with the swing ball at eye level.

At this point your vision and your brain will be well synchronized, and your vision process will be in its most relaxed mode.

Observations How well are you able to be aware of surrounding space while following the ball and playing the rest of the game?

Are you able to be so relaxed that each new level is viewed as a challenge and mastery soon occurs?

Do you feel dizzy, experience nausea, or have feelings of disorientation?

If your vision fitness is at a level where you decide to stay at one phase of the swing ball, do not feel that you have to master the next level right away. You will have three weeks and the rest of your life to master the higher levels.

At any point in the sequence go back to earlier vision games, and repeat them. Let your eyes tell you when to take a break. For example, if you feel frustrated during the swing ball game, take your patch off and palm your eyes. Notice whether this brings you back to the point where you feel relaxed enough to continue.

In this way you can be reviewing the previous days' activities while mastering the new ones.

Finally, you can transfer this new awareness into your daily life. When working on a particular project and you experience "blocks" in your ability to visually process, or the blur begins to influence your productivity or behavior, then put one or more of the vision games into action.

In this way, vision fitness becomes part of your routine. By the end of the three weeks, you will have mastered a set of new skills.

Week 1

Day 7 Shifting/Scanning

Purpose
To heighten your awareness that movement of the eyes leads to more relaxed and broader perception.

Instructions
This is the last vision game you will play using the one-eyed patch. Use the Eye-C chart, a book, a friend's face, look out of a window, or watch television.

Choose two points, one in the left, the other in the right part of your visual field. Let your eye shift back and forth between the two points as you breathe. Also add palming, soft focus, and zooming.

Feel what it is like to have the eye move in a relaxed way without any strain. This game will allow you to break any habitual patterns of staring or straining.

Repeat this for 20 breaths.

If you use someone's face, shift from earlobe to eyebrow, chin, nose, other eye, cheek, and so on. The eyes are actively moving.

This shifting is particularly helpful if you work at a computer. Shift between points on the screen while the computer is accessing data.

Computer users also place an Eye-C chart on walls or windows beyond or alongside their work stations. They very often zoom their eyes from the computer screen to the Eye-C chart to verify that their Eye-C is maintained. If the chart should become more blurry, then extend the time spent on palming.

The next phase is to introduce scanning or painting with the eyes open. Scanning is moving the eyes as in painting—however, without the imaginary paintbrush. Use the earlier painting game and begin scanning along the Eye-C chart, your friend's face, paintings, scenes out a window, the computer screen, or even your book. Unlike shifting, scanning is soft and gentle. In the beginning, you might find yourself holding your breath. The goal is to develop flow and ease while scanning.

Combine the feeling you mastered in soft focus and the awareness from the swing ball in shifting and scanning.

Repeat for five minutes per day or play two or three times during the day for shorter periods. As in other games, you may spend as much time as you like on this game while mastering it.

Observations Watch for shallow breathing and wanting to try too hard.

Observe your posture. I have noticed my patients tending to lean forward during this game.

Can you incorporate shifting/scanning to bring this new awareness into your daily life? Try using this game while standing in line, at the stoplight, on the train or bus, while cooking, cleaning your house, or even shaving or putting on make-up.

How is your performance on the Eye-C chart while you shift from the right side of the chart to the left?

If you gently scan each row of letters, paint them white, and allow the whiteness to come to your eyes, do you appreciate more details?

Shift from one row of letters to another.

Since letter charts ask you to perceive in two dimensions, you might begin straining. True balanced vision occurs when you see in three dimensions, so see the three-dimensionality of the Eye-C chart.

If your eyes are not moving, begin shifting and scanning.

Week 2

Day 8 Nose Pencil

Purpose   **T**o transfer the awareness of painting with the eyes closed into your open-eyed visual world.

Instructions   **P**lace your two-eyed patch on. Spend a few minutes walking around and adjusting to this new way of perceiving.

Notice whether you tend to look more out of one eye. If so, is that your preferred eye, which was covered during Week 1?

Adjust your head, if necessary, so you are looking out of the non-preferred eye. Now you can choose which eye you look out of under different conditions.

You might find it overly challenging to be looking through both eyes while doing book or desk work with the two-eyed patch in place. If so, look out of the non-preferred eye, and later, do activities that permit you to peep out of both eyes. Alternatively, make another two-eyed patch that is 1.5 millimeters shorter on each side. Use this patch for reading. You will find it easier to look out of both eyes with the narrower two-eyed patch.

The goal is to see a little out of the right eye and a little out of the left. If you align your head in exactly the right position, your sight will increase. This should easily be noticed on the Distance Eye-C chart.

Now recall the paint brush on the end of your nose. Conjure up an image of painting a picture white. I like to paint any unpleasant pictures white. When the picture is completely white, I imagine a pencil on the end of my nose. I open my eyes and pretend that the pencil can be made any color. I then look at a blank wall and paint a new, pleasant picture.

Then I sketch the corners of the room, objects seen through the window, and furniture or items on the walls.

The goal is to train your mind's eye to lead your physical eye.

Repeat the nose pencil game for five minutes per day.

Observations Can you zoom to different distances and use the nose pencil?

Become aware of straining or tension that may appear in the eyes or the muscles around them.

Introduce soft focus between sessions of the nose pencil game. While using the nose pencil also shift and scan!

Are certain things more difficult to sketch with the nose pencil than others?

Do you favor looking through one eye more than the other? Can you maintain looking through both eyes?

Week 2

Day 9 Lighting

Purpose To train your eyes and brain to enjoy light, and allow the light rays to heal your eyes.

Equipment Ideally, you would use the sun for this game. Under no circumstances should you look directly at the sun.

In many parts of the world the sun is only available for certain periods of the year, so the next best light source is a 60- or 100-watt Daylight Blue Color Corrected incandescent bulb (see Products For Seeing Beyond 20/20). The advantage of using this bulb is that the lighting vision game can be played inside and while you conduct your work at a desk.

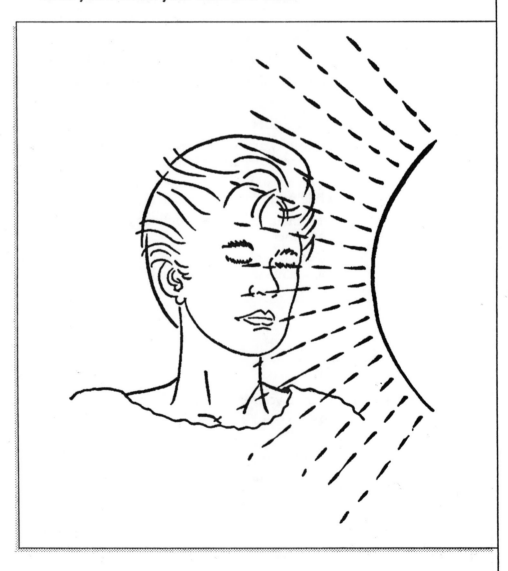

Place the bulb in a desk lamp that has a funnel shade, so you are not looking directly into the bulb when you are working.

Instructions If you are using the sun, stand or sit comfortably. Close your eyes and aim them toward the sun. You can perform this game the same way if you are using the light bulb.

The two-eyed patch will block some of the rays; however, the outer portions of your eyes will feel the warmth. This is particularly wonderful in the colder winter months.

While you are appreciating the warmth, imagine the white rays of light beaming down toward you. Imagine yourself being transparent and let the rays come to you. Picture all the colors of the spectrum: violet, indigo, blue, green, yellow, orange, and red.

Absorb the light and convert it to pictures of what you wish to see. (Recall your purpose and goals.) Let your eyeballs move slightly behind your closed lids. Now, take an imaginary journey to the coast on a warm sunny day. You might recall a time as a young child when you played on the beach in the sun with your parents.

Begin moving your head to the left and then the right. In this way each (closed) eye will in turn receive exposure to the light through the eyelid.

Imagine your third eye opening wide, like a flower slowly opening its bud, and you are receiving all the wavelengths of light beneficial for healing your eyes.

Pretend that the rays of light are traveling into your eyes and bouncing like rubber balls against your retina, stimulating the rods and cones.

Picture the little pineal gland, situated behind the third eye, receiving this healthy light. Just as a battery can be charged, let the pineal gland glow with a charge of any color you choose. Let that glow now flow outward in the form of seeing through the third eye.

As you experience the feeling of the glow, begin blinking your eyes once or twice as you rotate your head back and forth. Enjoy the light entering the eyes. Picture your pupil shutting down and opening up as you blink. Feel the iris muscle exercising as the pupil changes size.

Repeat for 50 to 100 breaths or more per day.

If you work at a computer, use this lighting game every other hour for a minute at a time.

Also, for this week, while wearing the two-eyed patch, read with one eye. Perhaps experiment by reading out of the non-preferred eye. Read a magazine or book in candle light that is placed about 13 to 16 inches from your eyes.

Stay particularly attentive to any strain; it will be the sign to stop reading and palm or zoom. Zoom onto the patch and then far away for 10 breaths. How does it feel to zoom as close as the patch? Do you feel pulling of the eye muscles?

Are both eyes turning in equally? Have your support person watch to supply the answer.

Observations As you master this game, you may find that your relationship with light changes. I personally found that I no longer grabbed for my sunglasses, particularly as I modified my intake of fatty and oily foods.

Lighting is particularly helpful for the two varieties of farsightedness. The farsightedness associated with age that affects your ability to read small print is called presbyopia. The lighting game will help keep the pupil small, which increases the depth of focus. In addition, the increase in contrast helps the ciliary muscle adjust its focus.

For the other, routine farsightedness, the lighting game will relax the strain on the focusing muscle.

Week 2

Day 10 Dynamic Visual Meditation (DVM)

Purpose   To train you to be relaxed and unfocused, and to visually let go while introducing body motion.

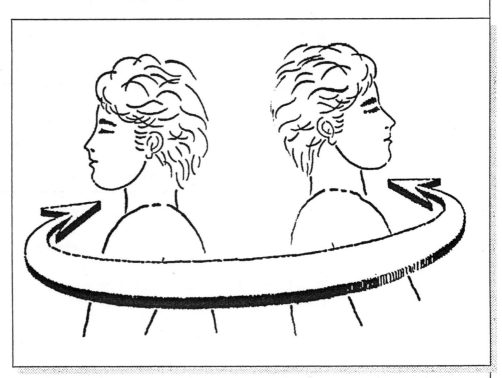

Instructions Wear comfortable and loose clothes. While wearing the two-eyed patch for this week, stand erect with your feet apart, equivalent to the width of your shoulders.

With your eyes closed begin rotating your shoulders, hips, and head to the left; all should move together. Repeat this movement to the right, then left again, until you are swinging back and forth. Allow your arms to swing freely and you may find them wrapping around your body as you turn. When going to the left, let the right foot turn with the heel coming up and out like a golf swing. Repeat for the right foot when swinging to the left. In the beginning, continue in this way for 10 minutes.

If you experience dizziness or falling over, check to see whether you are thinking. When you can produce a peacefulness in your mind, you will find your balance becomes perfect. Breathe and picture forests, mountains, or the ocean. Feel your body moving in a rhythmical way. Let go of all thoughts, like leaves falling off a tree in the fall.

When you have mastered this phase, focus your eyes on your eyelids. Begin to imagine that you can look outward through your closed eyelids. What would you see? Extend your vision beyond the two-eyed patch, still with closed eyelids.

Can you picture the room moving around as if you are riding a carousel horse at an amusement park? Imagine you can perceive the world zooming by as you play the dynamic visual meditation (DVM) game.

Extend your perception even further. Pretend that you have bionic or laser eyes and you can see through the walls. You can see across the city, the state, the country, the planet, into outer space.

All the time you are still moving your body back and forth with your eyes closed.

How far can you visualize before the picture becomes foggy or blurry?

Open your eyes and continue the DVM. At first pay attention to the patch as you swing. Attempt to look through the patch as you did with the closed eyelids. Gradually, begin to look around the sides of the patch.

The goal is to feel your eyes being perfectly still. Your eyes should move only in alignment with your head, shoulders, and hips.

Play the game in stages. It is important to master each stage before going on to the next.

Observations Have someone watch your eyes to make sure that there are no jerky eye movements.

If you feel strain or fatigue, paint white or shift and scan for a short time.

Begin to incorporate Week 1's games into the DVM.

I have found the *Brandenburg Concertos* by Bach to be a suitable tempo for this game. Experiment with different music.

How does the Eye-C chart appear with the two-eyed patch after this game? What happens to your looking and seeing if you remove the patch?

You cannot depend on your eyes when your imagination is out of focus.

—Mark Twain

Week 2

Day 11 Eye Muscle Stretch

Purpose   To master stretching the eye muscles to relieve tension while maintaining relaxation.

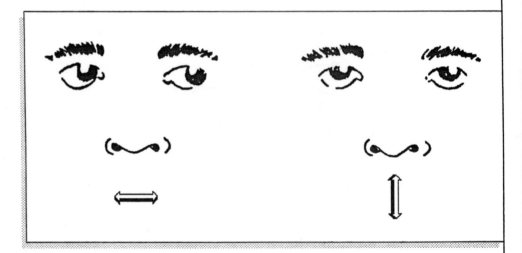

Instructions Seat yourself comfortably, wearing the two-eyed patch, with your hands supported on your lap and your feet relaxing squarely on the floor.

Take a few deep breaths, and then on one of the in-breaths, stretch your eyes upward. The goal is to stretch the eyes as high as they can go without straining.

Hold your breath and when you are ready to exhale, stretch the muscles into a downward position and breathe out. Repeat this up and down movement for three breaths. Then go left and right as well as up and to the left, and down and to the right. Be aware of your right visual field when you stretch to the right and vice versa.

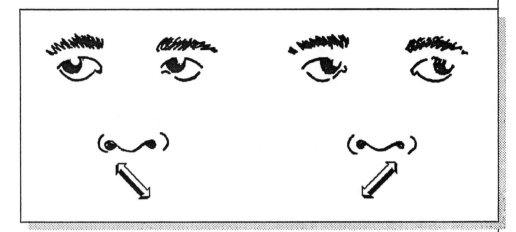

When you have mastered the above steps, let your eyes move around in circles; however, stretch the muscles to their extremities without straining. Your eyes should feel "alive" after three to five breaths of rotations in both directions.

Recall that vision fitness develops when the vision game is easy, without strain and tension. If you feel any tension, breathe a little more into the tightness. Avoid extreme stretching as this may produce additional strain.

When you have completed all the directions, reverse the breath; you will now breathe out as you stretch your eyes upward.

Remove the two-eyed patch and palm your eyes after this activity.

Repeat the eye muscle stretch three to six times during the day. You can stretch your eyes while you exercise, cook, watch television, read, work on the computer, stand in lines, and walk.

Observations As before, monitor your Eye-C after a stretching session. Squeeze your eyes gently closed after stretching.

In the beginning you may find particular places where there is tension in the muscles. As you play the game, you will find that the tension dissipates.

Week 2

Day 12 Marching

Purpose   To train your brain, eyes, and body to synchronize into whole-brain functioning.

Instructions Stand erect with your arms at your side, shoulders back and legs together.

Choose a point in space, preferably looking out through a window, with both eyes involved, seeing around the corners of the two-eyed patch.

Begin the game by imagining that you are a soldier. Let your left leg and left arm shoot out at the same time. Then repeat for the right side. Repeat this one-sided marching for 50 breaths. March at a pace equivalent to a brisk walk and coordinate your breathing.

When you have mastery, let the eyes move to the left when you move out the left limbs and vice versa. This may be challenging at first. Be patient and give yourself plenty of breaks.

When you have mastered this phase, begin humming a tune or song while you continue the vision game of marching. The goal is to be involved in the game in such a relaxed way that you can let your mind wander to the beach, the forests and mountains and not fall over!

Next, switch to a higher level: the left arm and right leg move out at the same time. This is the traditional reciprocal marching. In the beginning let the eyes look in front again. Then add the eye movements and lastly add the humming.

Observations Be brave and add spelling while marching.

I march on a small rebounder trampoline while looking out of my window watching the birds.

March in front of the Eye-C chart. Cross your eyes onto the patch and then look at the letters.

Paint white while you march.

By now you are realizing that the only limitation to having fun with the vision games is a lack of imagination.

Try to maintain your smooth marching while listening to distracting music, or have a friend attempt to distract you.

This game is particularly useful for developing vision fitness for dyslexics and the reading disabled.

Week 2

Day 13 Acupressure

Purpose   To stimulate the acupressure/acupuncture points by using pressure and massage from your fingers. (Acupressure involves stimulating nerve and energy points by applying pressure and movements of your fingers. Acupuncture is a similar process conducted by an acupuncturist. He/she inserts needles to accomplish the stimulation.)

Do not wear patches for this game.

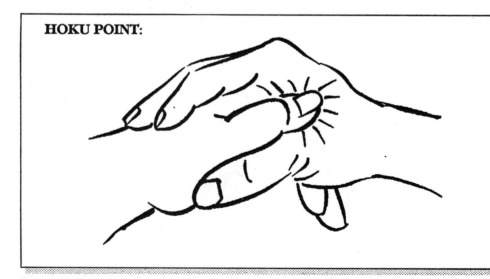

HOKU POINT:

Instructions Begin with the Hoku point (see page 133). The Hoku point is the cardinal point for the organs of the head and, of course, the eyes. According to my acupuncturist this point is good for relieving headaches.

Place the thumb and index finger of the left hand together. Locate the muscular hill of the right hand (see illustration). Separate the index finger and thumb of the left hand. Place the left-hand thumb on the muscular hill. Position the left index finger on the inside of the right palm corresponding to the point of the muscular hill.

Increase the pressure of the thumb and index finger against each other. You will be applying pressure to the Hoku point. Stimulate each hand for 10 to 20 breaths.

The Eyebrow/Thumb point has proven helpful for enhancing Eye-C performance.

EYEBROW THUMB POINT:

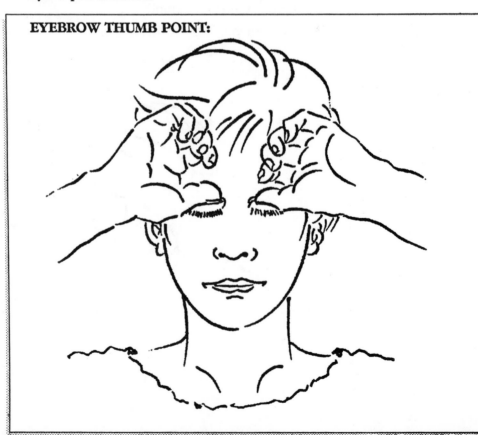

Use your thumbs to massage or apply pressure to the inside eyebrow corners. Add pressure to this point until the first feeling of discomfort. The other fingers can be placed on the forehead.

The Nose point is stimulated by using the thumb and index finger over the nose bridge. Stimulating this point relieves the pressure build-up due to straining.

NOSE POINT:

The Temple point is found in a hollow on the side of the head. Massaging this point relieves headaches or pressure in the temples. Place your index fingers on both temples and locate the hollow space. Apply pressure and massage this point for 10 to 20 breaths.

TEMPLE POINT:

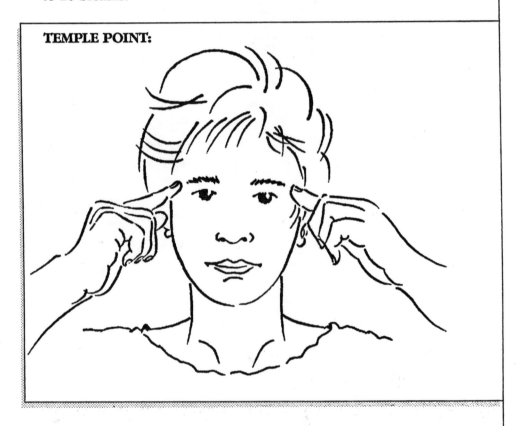

With your fingers and thumbs massage the Eyebrow/Cheek point. Follow the directions in the diagram. Stimulating the forehead relieves tightness due to eye straining. Massaging the cheek point clears the sinuses and your breathing becomes easier.

EYEBROW POINT:

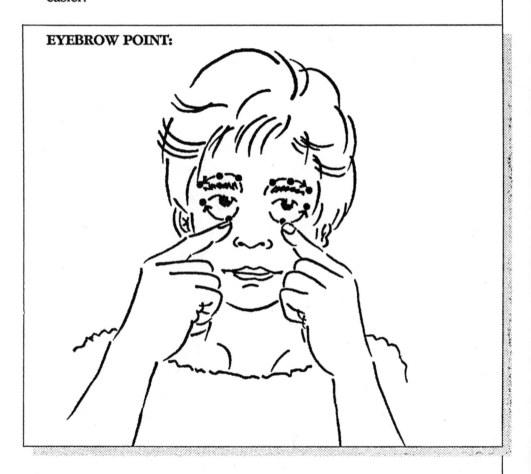

Observations Combine the acupressure game with the Eye-C chart.

Find a point that is most effective for you in relieving tension.

How is your general disposition after the game?

Week 2

Day 14 Shoulder and Neck Massage

Purpose   To relieve tension and improve blood and nerve flow to the eyes.

Instructions Ideally, this vision game is performed with the assistance of a support person.

When you are playing on your own, place the left hand over the right shoulder. Using your four fingers, massage the shoulder muscle. Concentrate on the muscle that is near the neck and work your way outward.

Breathe and look into the distance while performing the massage.

After a while let your neck roll a few times, making a circle.

Repeat the same process with your right hand over the left shoulder.

The back of the neck in general and one particular area, felt as two bumps or ridges, is another acupressure point related to vision.

Place your thumbs onto the two ridges at the back of your head. Let the rest of your fingers relax on your head. Put as much pressure on the ridges, or underneath them, as you can tolerate.

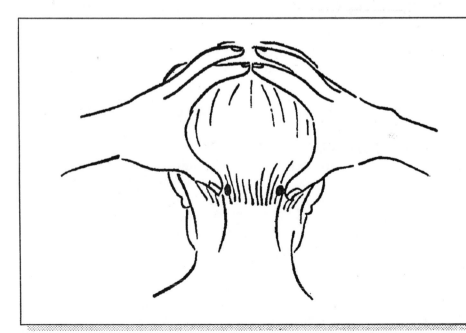

Watch the Eye-C chart and you will enjoy the flashes of clarity.

Repeat for 20 to 50 breaths. If at work, play this game for five breaths every couple of hours.

Observations How do you feel after a few minutes of massage?

How is your Eye-C? Is it clear at first and then blurry? Can you bring the clearness back? Do you notice a difference in the Eye-C chart when you remove the two-eyed patch?

Combine the eye muscle stretch with this game.

Do your favorite acupressure points.

What combination of games produces the most exciting results for you?

Week 3

Day 15
String Thing (Note: No patch is worn when playing the games this week!)

Purpose To train each eye's perception to be accepted by the brain, and to cooperate in "whole-brain" perceiving.

Materials 10-foot string with three colored beads that can slide along the string.

Instructions Attach one end of the string to a door handle or other fixture. You can also use a screw-in hook connected to any wooden surface. I have seen string things attached above beds, on verandahs, in bathrooms and in kitchens. The most ingenious setup I have seen is the string tied to a TV!

Pull the string tight and place the other end on the tip of your nose. Make sure that your finger doesn't block the vision from either eye.

Place one of the wooden beads, say the red, at the far end next to the knot or point of attachment. The next bead, the blue, is placed halfway down the string, while the green is brought to your optimum close distance (the point where you can just make out the detail of the bead; this distance will vary depending on

whether you are farsighted or nearsighted). If the close bead becomes unclear, move it closer or farther away until it clears. Focus your attention (looking) at the closest green bead. With both eyes open, and relaxed breathing, get in touch with how your eyes feel while looking at the bead.

Can you see one bead or does it slip into two images? Do you feel any strain or tension in your eye muscles? While looking at the closest bead can you see what is going on behind that bead?

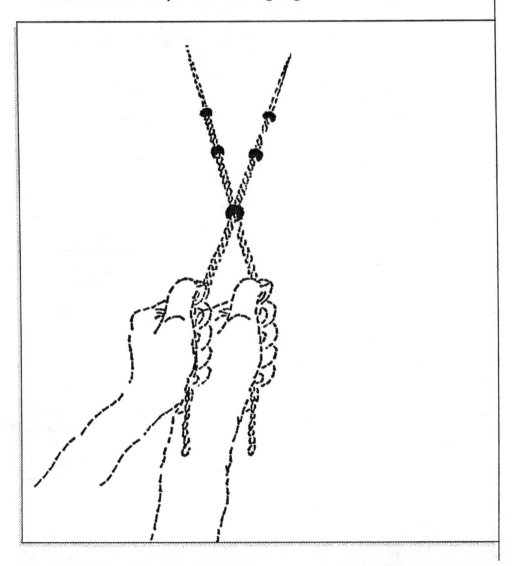

The answers to these questions will assist you in understanding your level of vision fitness.

If you can balance your looking and seeing, you will notice that the distant beads appear double.

You may also see two strings radiating from the near bead in both directions. These are good signs. They mean that both eyes are working together and the brain is accepting both images.

If any parts of the string disappear, then parts of visual space are being suppressed. This could mean that your subconscious is not wanting to see part of what is in your world.

If any of the distant beads disappear, this indicates the brain cannot simultaneously handle inputs from both eyes.

Attempt to bring the near bead closer to your nose. If you can maintain one bead image, your vision fitness is good. If the bead begins slipping into two, then play the game more often, until you achieve mastery.

String Thing is an excellent game to play with pre-school children, to prepare them for learning to read.

You could use String Thing to verify your vision fitness after working at a computer terminal.

Play the game for 20 to 30 breaths, then zoom to other beads, and finally palm.

Observations Under what conditions do the beads or parts of the string disappear?

When you incorporate spelling, talking, or thinking, what happens to the string(s) or the beads? Let your mind wander for a moment. Now what happens?

Zoom back and forth between the different beads. Maintain one bead where you are "looking" and two beads where you "see"!

Close your eyes and imagine the position of the beads. In your mind's eye zoom back and forth between the beads.

Do you experience more stamina after playing the game?

Week 3

Day 16 Fencing

Purpose   To extend the concepts learned on Day 15 into space and your daily life. To train your brain and eyes to simultaneously look and see.

Materials   A 32-inch piece of flexible, plastic-covered electrical wire.

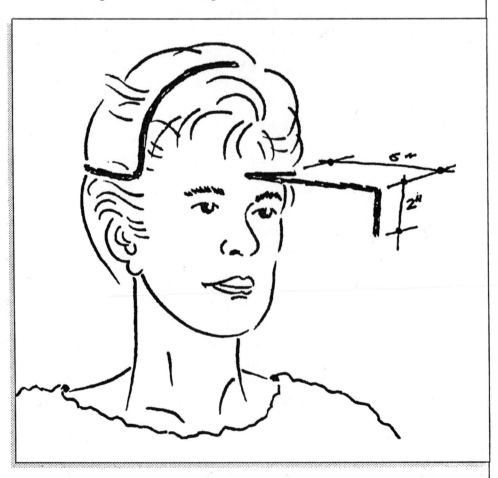

Instructions   Bend the wire following the sketch example to custom-fit your head. The goal is to have a piece of wire hanging in front of your eyes at about six inches. This wire is called the fence post for this game.

As in the String Thing, when you look past the single fence post, observe that there now appear two! Whatever you are looking at, place that object of regard exactly between the fence posts.

Make sure that both fence posts are present all the time. If not, blink your eyes, take a deep breath, aim your eyes toward the single fence post and then relax. The second fence post should return. If it doesn't, remove the gadget and palm your eyes, stretch the muscles, massage the face, and yawn. Repeat until you see two posts. *(NOTE: Should you be unable to elicit two fence posts, then your vision fitness may be too low for you to master fencing at this time. Continue working on earlier games until your vision fitness increases.)* Walk around the room placing objects between the fence posts. The goal, as before, is to be able to look and see! What you look at appears single and what you see appears double.

Look out of a window and imagine in your mind's eye that you can see across the street, the other side of the city, outside your state, across country.

As you pretend looking at a far distance and imagine a clear object in that place, notice what happens to the separation of the fence posts.

Visualize that looking farther into space is equivalent to creating more visual space. This is monitored by how far apart you see the fence posts. The farther you look, the greater separation between the fence posts. The farther they separate, the more space there is.

As in the String Thing, imagine there is a string coming from the object in far space stretching out toward the real (single) fence post.

When you are looking right at the fence post, the two posts will merge into one fence post, and your eyes will be crossing. Remember, it is fine to cross your eyes—they will not get stuck—as long as you do not strain.

There is no time limit to playing Fencing.

Observations How does it feel to look at the fence post and see one?

If there is any tension or strain, breathe, blink, and palm your eyes for 20 to 50 breaths.

Use the fencing game while you watch TV, read, cook, talk with friends, and work at the computer.

Become aware under what conditions the two fence posts change. Notice when one fence post fades, becomes blurry, moves, or disappears. Observe whether you want to avoid looking between the two fence posts under certain viewing conditions.

Fencing is a wonderful way to monitor how thinking, distress, and tension affect the working of the two eyes together.

Week 3

**Day 17
Thumb
Zapping**   See Chapter 11 for a detailed description of this game.

Week 3

Day 18 Finger Doubling

Purpose   To induce beginning awareness of stereoscopic perception and further develop "whole-brain" vision.

Instructions Place your two thumbs, one behind the other, at 10 inches in front of your eyes.

While looking far away perceive two thumbs.

Now place one thumb next to the other thumb and slightly separate them to a distance of about two inches.

Keep looking far away and notice that you will now see either four or three thumbs.

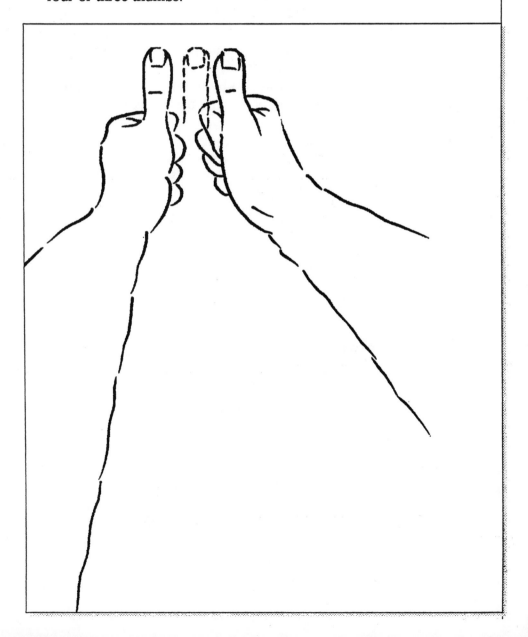

Separate the physical thumbs a little further until you are aware of three thumbs. Keep breathing and blinking to maintain a balanced perception of the three thumbs.

Now zoom your looking to the point where you think there are three thumbs, and you will notice that they go back into two.

Zoom far away and there will once again be three. Practice this zooming until it is easy for you to see three thumbs even while standing on one leg.

Move your two physical thumbs farther away and closer, and observe the effect this has on your ability to maintain three thumbs.

The next step in finger doubling is to cross your eyes slightly. By crossing your eyes you will either see four or three thumbs. The goal is to see three and to make the middle thumb as clear as possible.

Place your physical thumbs at different distances from your face and notice how your performance varies.

Next, see if you can again look past the physical thumbs and perceive three. Attempt to zoom behind and in front, getting three thumbs each time.

Spend 15 minutes if necessary to gain mastery.

Observations Spell different words while zooming to different distances.

Sit in front of the Eye-C chart and notice changes while you zoom and see three thumbs.

Include plenty of palming, pressure points, and yawns.

Week 3

Day 19
Circles   See Chapter 11 for a detailed description of this game.

Week 3

Day 20 Imaging

Purpose   To train your inner vision to create pictures of anything you desire.

Instructions Find a quiet place where you can play the imaging game.

The first step is to make yourself very relaxed. Enjoy five deep breaths.

Imagine yourself at your current age. See your home, animals, bedroom, and kitchen. See the colors of the walls, your view out of different windows.

Imagine a trip you took last summer. Experience the pictures in vivid colors. Pretend you can feel objects that you see.

Hear yourself talking to friends, family members, and colleagues.

Go back to any age and repeat the same game.

How well can you see your parents? Can you see them sharing themselves with you? Do you feel love coming from them? Can you pretend that your parents are loving you now?

Begin to see yourself without your eyeglasses or contacts. What would your experience of seeing without eyeglasses be like? How soon can you imagine that happening?

See yourself as a child without eyeglasses.

Image the period about 18 months prior to receiving eyeglasses. How much distress did you have during this period? Let your mind's eye create any pictures you desire of the past, present, or future.

Observations How easy is it for you to imagine? Can you let your mind just "free flow"? Can you quiet the conscious mind enough to see pictures?

How well can you write about your imaging experience?

How does the imaging game connect to your goals or purpose?

Week 3

Day 21 Maintenance Program

Purpose To review the whole program and decide how you can incorporate the most effective components into your daily life.

Instructions By reading your diary and recalling the most effective vision games, begin a list of the activities that you would like to continue. The maintenance program can include relaxation, an imagery tape, patches, vision games, nutrition, aerobic exercise, affirmations, and record keeping.

You may wish to use the Eye-C chart once a week and patches for specific activities like reading, bookkeeping, or working on the computer.

When during the day could you include your favorite vision games? By the end of this day, you should have a master list outlining how you intend to continue your *Seeing Beyond 20/20* program.

Observations How effective are you in keeping up the program?

Are you seeking follow-up care with your eye doctor?

When do you intend to obtain your next reduced lens prescription?

Do you have a friend who might wish to repeat the 21-day program with you in the future?

EPILOGUE: WORLD'S-EYE VIEW

The African Bushmen, prior to the Coca-Cola bottle experience, led a very peaceful life. Little conflict existed between the members of the tribe. Similarly, animals left to roam the wilds are calm. Contrast this with Blacks oppressed by Apartheid, animals locked up in cages, and persons having to conform to a military government.

Natural seeing can be blocked by fear and anger responses to environmental or social pressures. Because this is happening around the world—witness the constant battles between Arabs and Jews, and Protestants and Catholics, not to mention the Cold War of America and Russia—it's not surprising that a defensive way of looking at life develops. It would appear that biases and judgments stemming from fear or anger can precipitate an imbalance of whole-brain processing.

I recall recently seeing a *Newsweek* photograph of rioting Blacks in South Africa. The most striking aspect of the photograph was the hatred and anger radiating from their eyes.

I have often wondered, what would happen if the leaders of our countries around the world looked through vision fitness lenses? Would the world be a different place if more of us used our highest level of natural vision fitness?

My personal experience is that using natural perception, as opposed to looking through filters of bias, racial prejudice, greed for power and wealth, and political dominance, produces a calm, peaceful vision of now and the future. It's my strongest desire that the principles, theories, techniques, and suggestions presented here will move the world to *Seeing Beyond 20/20*.

"Wherever you look, see love and peace!"

The following clinical research was conducted at Pacific University's Portland Optometric Clinic during the fall of 1982. These research findings were reported in a paper presented at the 1982 Annual Meeting of The American Academy of Optometry in Chicago. Dr. Brian Henson collaborated in the compilation of the statistical findings.

Subject Selection

Subjects for the clinical investigation were chosen by random selection from respondents to a newspaper advertisement and word of mouth. Potential subjects were screened by undertaking an optometric examination to find current levels of refractive error, muscle balance, stereopsis, and amounts of presbyopia, if any. (Only myopic and presbyopic subjects were chosen for the study.)

Subjects were given written and verbal information about the purpose of the study, the time involved, and the commitments they needed to make. The optometric measurements were made by optometric interns supervised by clinical optometrists. At the time of the testing, neither the interns nor the subjects knew whether candidates were part of an experimental or control group.

The investigator randomly chose participants for the experimental group and brought them together for a weekend orientation. At that point they were informed of being the experimental group. The orientation included explanations of the human visual system, the difference between sight and vision, use of affirmations, nutrition and vision, aerobic and movement exercise, self-relaxation audio tapes, use of Eye-C charts, and home vision games. Each subject was given a manual, which contained much of the content of *Seeing Beyond 20/20*, and all of the vision games presented in the format of the 21 days.

The subjects were given forms on which to record their daily food consumption, exercise schedules, Eye-C chart results, and guidelines for maintaining a commitment to the program. The subjects filled out the Vision Fitness Questionnaire and the Visual Style Ratings as presented in the text of the book.

Subjects were then divided into teams with designated team leaders. These teams acted as support groups throughout the 21-day period. Any subject could call a team leader at any time to report problems or concerns. The teams met once a week to report challenges and any other insights or experiences to the team leader, who then called the investigator. In this way there was constant communication between the subjects and researcher. Any major problems or misunderstandings could be dealt with immediately.

The 21 Days

The 21-day program was divided into three one-week periods. The first week was devoted to monocular vision. Subjects wore a patch over one eye for up to four hours per day during their daily routine as long as they felt they were in a safe environment. They played the vision games daily, adding a new game each day.

Besides the games, they were taught to perform breathing and relaxation techniques.

In week two, the subjects were introduced to two-eyed viewing. Individual custom-made bi-nasal (two-eyed) patches were provided and worn during the games. New games were added to the first week's program. All the games were able to be performed without instrumentation and were easily understood.

The third week was devoted entirely to two-eyed vision. One binocular game was added each day to the previous two weeks' games.

During the three-week period, the subjects kept track of their food intake, aerobic exercise, Eye-C measurements, daily goals, and personal experiences. At the completion of the three weeks, the subjects turned in all their records and set up appointments for the post-testing.

Results

For the post-testing, the experimental and control group subjects came in for testing at the same time. Optometric interns again undertook the testing without knowing which group the subject was in. Table I shows the breakdown of the control and experimental groups in terms of age, education level, and numbers (n) of myopic and presbyopic subjects.

Table I
Subject Data

	Control	Experimental
Numbers (n)	21	62
Age (Mean)	37	34.7
Min. Age	25	14
Max. Age	64	60
Educational Level		
<H.S.		1.7%
H.S.		11.7%
>H.S.		25.%
B.A., B.S.		41.6%
>B.S.		6.7%
M.A., M.S.		6.7%
>M.S.		6.7%
Myopes	15	50
Presbyopes	6	12

Table II shows the clinical data of the control and experimental groups. The stereopsis and fixation disparity measurements were made with the American Optical Vectograph Slide, polaroid filters, and loose prisms at far and near.

Table II
Data of Experimental Group and Control Group

Test	Control				Experimental			
	n	$\overline{X}$b	$\overline{X}$a	t	n	$\overline{X}$b	$\overline{X}$a	t
V.A. @ far unaided	17	20/75	20/66	.88	44	20/105	20/77	3.877*
Stereopsis through habitual Rx	18	138"	126"	-.638	48	206"	156"	3.15*
Range of prism diopters to fixation disparity @ far	18	4.58	4.5	.09	45	5.2	7.48	-5.38*
Range of prism diopters to fixation disparity @ near	18	6.82	8.65	-1.55	45	7.58	9.02	-2.76*
Vision Fitness Score	20	7.55	8.85	-1.37	58	5.82	9.67	-7.17*
% wearing time of 20/20 Rx#					40	78.9%	19.2%	11.66*

$\overline{X}$b = before

$\overline{X}$a = after

* = Significant level of at least .05 using two-tailed test and five planned tests

= unplanned test

The results show that for the experimental group, visual acuity at far, stereopsis at far, and range of prism diopters around the fixation disparity at far and near all changed for the better between pre- and post-testing. All other optometric data for either group did not change for the better between the two testings.

The vision fitness score derived from the questionnaire also changed very significantly for the experimental group. The subjects were asked to record the wearing time of their current eyeglasses during the 21 days. It was found that the percentage wearing time dropped from 78.9 percent to 19.2 percent—a significant drop in their eyeglass dependency.

Table III shows the breakdown of the myopic group and the presbyopic group. This shows that the presbyopes as a group did not show any significant changes. They had the same tendencies for improvements as did the group as a whole, but not at an experimentally significant level. Perhaps a larger sample size would reflect these trends.

Table III
Experimental Group Data for Myopes and Presbyopes

Test	Myopes				Presbyopes			
	n	$\overline{X}b$	$\overline{X}a$	t	n	$\overline{X}b$	$\overline{X}a$	t.
V.A. @ far unaided	36	20/110	20/77	3.12*	11	20/68	20/61	2.5
V.A. @ near unaided	36	20/26	20/27	.988	8	20/35	20/34	-.32
Stereopsis through habitual Rx	40	194"	150"	2.51	8	240"	187.5"	-1.87
Range of prism diopters to fixation disparity @ far	39	5.1	7.5	-5.18*	6	6	7.7	-1.41
Range of prism diopters to fixation disparity @ near	37	7.82	9.12	2.44	8	6.5	8.56	-1.3
Vision fitness score	40	5.87	9.98	-7.95*	12	7.75	9.17	-2.05

$\overline{X}b$ = mean pre score
$\overline{X}a$ = mean post score
* = significant level of at least .05 using two-tailed test and five planned tests

Table IV shows a percentage change from pre- to post-testing from a behavioral questionnaire given to the subjects. They were rated on a scale of 1 to 10 with 1 being a behavior never noticed, and 10 something they did constantly.

Table IV
Behaviors

List of behaviors that changed significantly from pre- to post-testing. Each of the listed behaviors was given at least a 5 on the rating scale. See text for explanation of rating scale. Pre and post refer to the number of subjects who reported the particular behavior.

Behavior	Pre	Post	% change
1. Skip word or sentences	22	13	41
2. Reread lines or phrases	30	14	53
3. Read too slowly	22	13	41
4. Comprehension poorer as reading is continued or loses interest quickly	15	7	53
5. Headaches in forehead or temples	14	7	50
6. Frowns, scowls or squints	20	14	30
7. Rest head on arm when writing	5	11	55
8. Write crookedly and/or poorly spaced	12	7	42

Summary

The *Seeing Beyond 20/20* three-week program demonstrated that when subjects were supported in applying an interdisciplinary approach to developing vision, they could produce significant changes in their perception as measured by binocular optometric measurements.

The refractive data did not change significantly; however, the positive increase in ranges around the fixation disparity can be interpreted as greater tolerance for handling visual stress. This seemed to be confirmed by the behavioral comments from the research subjects.

Behaviors related to general vision skills and fitness of the visual processing system improved by the time of post-testing. These findings suggest that the visual performance of eye movements, focusing, and binocularity can change in a short home-based vision training program like the 21-day *Seeing Beyond 20/20* program.

Conclusions

Since so many variables—nutrition, relaxation, patches, exercise, vision games, support, affirmations, and others—together produced the significant changes, future studies should determine which of the variables affect the changes. Is it possible that the holistic approach as outlined in *Seeing Beyond 20/20* is necessary for the overall "whole-person" shifts? Control group subjects were later taken through exactly the same experimental program without the dedicated support, and their findings did not change significantly. These subjects were less inclined to comply with such requirements as sticking to the nutritional and exercise suggestions. Future studies can investigate this further.

The 21-day program clearly demonstrated that when persons are adequately trained and supervised, they can execute a home-based vision fitness program. It is my desire that such home-based programs be taught to our children so that they, the future generation, can attain the highest levels of vision fitness possible. Perhaps this will permit them to see beyond 20/20.

SELECT BIBLIOGRAPHY

Anderson, A. *How the Mind Heals.* Psychology Today 51-56, December, 1982.

Aronsfeld, G. H. *Eyesight Training and Development.* J. Am. Optom. Assoc. 7(4): 36-38, 1936.

Baldwin, W. R. *A Review of Statistical Studies of Relations Between Myopia and Ethnic, Behavioral, and Psychological Characteristics.* Am. J. Optom. Physiol. Opt. 58(7): 516-27, 1981.

Balliet, R.; Clay, A.; and Blood, K. *The Training of Visual Acuity in Myopia.* J. Am. Optom. Assoc. 53(9): 719-24, 1982.

Beach, G.; and Kavner, R. S. *Conjoint Therapy: A Cooperative Psychotherapeutic-Optometric Approach to Therapy.* J. Am. Optom. Assoc. 48(12): 1501-08, 1977.

Bell, G. *A Review of the Sclera and Its Role in Myopia.* J. Am. Optom. Assoc. 49: 1399-1403, 1978.

Bell, G. R. *The Coleman Theory of Accommodation and Its Relevance to Myopia.* J. Am. Optom. Assoc. 51(6): 582-87, 1980.

Birnbaum, M. H. *Holistic Aspects of Visual Style: A Hemispheric Model With Implications for Vision Therapy.* J. Am. Optom. Assoc. 49(10): 1133-41, 1978.

Dowis, R. T. *The Effect of a Visual Training Program on Juvenile Delinquency.* J. Am. Optom. Assoc. 48(9): 1173-76, 1193-94, 1977.

Forest, E. *Functional Vision: Its Impact on Learning.* J. Optom. Vis. Devel. 13(2): 12-15, 1982.

Francke, A. W.; and Carr, W. K. *Culture and the Development of Vision.* J. Am. Optom. Assoc. 47(1): 14-41, 1976.

Friedman, E. *Vision Training Program for Myopia Management.* Am. J. Optom. Physiol. Opt. 58(7): 546-53, 1981.

Gil, K. M.; and Collins, F. L. *Behavioral Training for Myopia: Generalization of Effects.* Behavior Res. Ther. 21(3): 269-73, 1983.

Goss, D. A. *Attempts to Reduce the Rate of Increase of Myopia in Young People: A Critical Literature Review.* Am. J. Optom. Physiol. Opt. 59(10): 828-41, 1982.

Gottlieb, R. L. *Neuropsychology of Myopia.* J. Optom. Vis. Devel. 13(1): 3-27, 1982.

Graham, C.; and Leibowitz, H. W. *The Effect of Suggestion on Visual Acuity.* Int. J. Clin. and Exp. Hypnosis 20(3): 169-86, 1972.

Greenspan, S. B. *1979 Annual Review of Literature in Developmental Optometry.* J. Optom. Vis. Devel. 10(1): 12-74, 1979.

Harris, P. A. *Myopia Control in China.* Opt. Extension Program 53, 1981.

Kaplan, R.-M. *Hypnosis, New Horizons for Optometry.* Rev. Optom. 115(10): 53-58, 1978.

Kaplan, R.-M. *Orthoptics or Surgery? A Case Report.* Optom. Weekly 68(39): 33-36, 1977.

Kaplan, R.-M. *Changes in Form Visual Fields in Reading Disabled Children Produced by Syntonic (Colored Light) Stimulation.* The Int. J. Of Biosocial Res. 5(1): 20-33, 1983.

Kappel, G. *Cataract Prevention and Cure Research.* Opt. Extension Program 52, 1980.

Kelley, C. R. *Psychological Factors in Myopia.* J. Am. Optom. Assoc. 33(6): 833-37, 1962.

Kirshner, A. J. *Visual Training and Motivation.* J. Am. Optom. Assoc. 38(8): 641-45, 1967.

Kruger, P. B. *The Effect of Cognitive Demand on Accommodation.* Am. J. Optom. Physiol. Opt. 57(7): 440-45, 1980.

Lane, B. *Nutrition and Vision.* J. Optom. Vis. Devel. 11(3): 1-11, 1980.

BIBLIOGRAPHY OF SUGGESTED READINGS

Aihara, Herman. *Basic Macrobiotics*. Tokyo and New York: Japan Publications, Inc., 1985.

Albert, Rachel. *Gourmet Whole Foods: Vegetarian and Macrobiotic Cuisine*. Grain of Salt Publishing, 2211 N.E. 50th, Suite 12, Seattle, WA 98105, 1986.

Brown, Barbara. *Super Mind*. Harper Row, 1980.

Buzan, Tony. *Using Both Sides of Your Brain*. New York: E. P. Dutton, 1974.

Coca, Arthur. *The Pulse Test*. New York: Arco, 1978.

Cooper, Kenneth. *The Aerobics Way*. New York: M. Evans and Co., 1977.

Delacato, Carl H. *The Treatment and Prevention of Reading Problems*. Springfield, Illinois: Charles C. Thomas, 1959.

Edwards, Betty. *Drawing on the Right Side of the Brain*. Los Angeles: Tarcher, 1979.

Franck, Frederick. *The Zen of Seeing*. New York: Vintage Books, 1973.

Gold, Svea. *When Children Invite Child Abuse: A Search for Answers When Love Is Not Enough*. Eugene, Oregon: Fern Ridge Press, 1986.

Goldberg, Stephen. *The Four-Minute Neurological Exam*. Medmaster, 1984.

Goodrich, Janet. *Natural Vision Improvement*. Berkeley, California: Celestial Arts, 1986.

Huxley, Aldous. *The Art of Seeing*. Seattle, Washington: Montana Books, 1975.

Kime, Zane. *Sunlight Could Save Your Life*. Penryn, California: World Health Publication, 1985.

Lowen, Alexander. *Bioenergetics*. Penguin Books, 1975.

Mendelsohn, Robert. *Confessions of a Medical Heretic*. Chicago: Contemporary Books, 1979.

Ott, John. *Health and Light*. Old Greenwich, Connecticut: Devin-Adair, 1973.

Ott, John. *Light, Radiation and You*. Old Greenwich, Connecticut: Devin-Adair, 1982.

Ponder, Catherine. *Dynamic Laws of Prosperity*. Prentice Hall, 1962.

Ray, Sondra. *Loving Relationships*. Millbrae, California: Celestial Arts, 1980.

Rotte, Joanna and Koji Yamamoto. *Vision: A Holistic Guide to Healing the Eyesight*. New York: Japan Publications, 1986.

Samuels, Michael and Nancy. *Seeing With the Mind's Eye*. New York: Random House, 1975.

Scholl, Lisette. *Visionetics*. New York: Doubleday, 1978.

Simonton, Carl O. *Getting Well Again*. Bantam Books, 1980.

Smotherman, Ron. *Winning Through Enlightenment*. San Francisco: Context Publications, 1980.

Vissel, Joyce and Barry. *Models of Love: The Parent-Child Journey*. Aptos, California: Ramira Publishing, 1986.

PRODUCTS FOR SEEING BEYOND 20/20

A. *Patches* (Black or white foam backed with elastic; adult or child size)
1. Adult $4
2. Child $2

B. *Daylight Blue Color Corrected Incandescent Light Bulbs* (Excellent for reading and for use in the Lighting vision game; provides illumination to the work surface at the computer terminal; rated for 3000 user hours)
1. 100 Watt $10.50
2. 60 Watt $8.50

C. 30-day supply of *Nova Multi-Vitamin/Mineral Food Supplements* (Formulated by a chiropractor; conveniently packaged, sustained released and combined with herbs and digestive enzymes). Consult with Dr. Kaplan on other food programs for specific eye conditions.
....$25

D. *Custom-Made Consultation Audio Tape* (Dr. Kaplan will conduct a personal 1/2 hour consultation on tape for your specific condition after you fill out an in-depth questionnaire or write to him with particular questions.)
....$45

E. *"Relax and See" Self-Guided Imagery Audio Tape* (Used in the Seeing Beyond 20/20 research studies. A tape you listen to before going to sleep. Has affirmations and guided imagery — very relaxing.)
....$9.95

F. *Seeing Beyond 20/20 "21-Day Vision Games"* on four audio tapes (Narrated by Dr Kaplan). Excellent way to integrate the vision games in your subconscious so you can then apply them into your daily life.
....$39.95

ORDER FORM

Circle the products you wish to purchase

A1   A2   B1   B2   C   D   E   F

Please specify the quantities

____   ____   ____   ____   ____   ____   ____   ____

Name (please print)

Address

City   State   Zip   Phone #

Enclose a check or money order and include $2.50 for postage and handling to Eye Fitness™ Systems, 401 S.W. 11th Avenue, Portland, OR 97205, USA.

Visa and MasterCard accepted # _____ Exp. date _____

Name on card _____

For credit card orders, call 1-800-444-2020 and leave ordering info.

RESOURCES

Association For Children And Adults With Learning Disabilities
4156 Library Road
Pittsburgh, PA 15234
(Parent/teacher support and network organization)

College Of Optometrists In Vision Development
353 H St., Suite C
Chula Vista, CA 92010
(Referral for optometrists who provide vision therapy services)

Optometric Extension Program Foundation, Inc.
2912 South Daimler St.
Santa Ana, CA 92705
(Optometrists interested in functional vision)

National Health Federation
P. O. Box 688
Monrovia, CA 91016
(Political and educational organization interested in protecting the health rights of the public)

American Optometric Association
243 N. Lindberg Blvd.
St. Louis, MO 63141
(Most active organization for the optometric profession)

E 9

B C 8

F D L 7

P T E O 6

Z B F D E 5

L C T B F O 4

P E O F D L Z 3

O Z B T D F C E 2

B L D E C Z O F F 1

E   100

B C   50

F D L   35

P T E O   25

Z B F D E   20

L C T B F O   15

P E O F D L Z   10

O Z B T D F C E   7.5

B L D E C Z O P F   5

"Turning-in" game, 25-26

20/20 vision: definition of, 10-11; improving vision in 20/20 sighted patients, 36, 64

21-Day Program
—components: affirmations, 85-87; eating plan, 90-91; exercise plan, 92; goal-setting, 79-84, 97; natural light, 93; patches, 94-96; relaxation, 88-89; vision games, 96-98, 103, 104-49
—introduction, 76-78
—summary of components, 78
—Vision fitness exercises for specific eye parts, 27

Vision fitness. *See also* Biofeedback use of eyes; Coordination, two-eyed; Mind's-eye perception; Visual style
—applications of approach, XII
—clarity of seeing and, 2-3; 95-96
—and eye-brain connection, 62
—information processing: symptoms of breakdown in, 4
—loss of: contributing factors, 7-10, 12, 21-22, 28, 32-33, 34-36, 44-50, 51-55, 57-60; and reading problems, 2, 28-29; statistics on, VII, 7, 8; symptoms, VII, IX, 2-6, 8-9; and 20/20 vision, 2, 4, 8, 15
—multiple personalities and, 59
—lenses (reduced power): optimum prescription for, 12, 13, 14; and suppressed emotions, 60; use to enhance vision fitness, 3, 12, 45; use to monitor vision fitness, 12-16, 40; and visual style, 33
—maintenance techniques, 12-13, 16
—monitoring of, 12-16, 35, 40
—vision fitness percentage: definition of, 10-11; and foveal focus, 24; and nutrition, 35-36, 40

Vision fitness questionnaire, 4-6

Vision games. *See* 21-day program

Visual mapping game, 59

A FINAL NOTE FROM THE AUTHOR

Since the first edition of *Seeing Beyond 20/20*, I have received many letters from all over the world from satisfied users of the program. As a result, I have offered *Seeing Beyond 20/20* educational programs in Holland, Switzerland, Germany, Israel, New Zealand, Australia, England, USA and Canada to further assist persons develop vision fitness, and provide Eye Fitness™ Practitioner Training Programs.

The purpose of the programs is to deepen the experiences of the dynamic relationship between vision and behavior. In addition, by adding the visual science to natural vision methods, the learning process is broadened and aligned with the philosophy of Behavioral Optometry.

My intention is to continue providing vision education and certify qualified persons to teach *Seeing Beyond 20/20*.

The curriculum includes the study of:
- Trampolining and developing visual behavior
- The role of imagery in visual healing
- Integrating spiritual vision and outer sight
- Designing daily programs and preparing foods for enhancing vision
- Managing computer eyestrain
- Advanced therapeutic lens prescriptions
- Steps to releasing limiting perceptions and blind spots
- Movement activities for unleashing balanced vision
- Audio-visual programs for opening visualization abilities
- Developing language and affirmations for reinforcing new visual habits
- Specific visual healing education for eye conditions including glaucoma, cataracts, iritis, macular degeneration, retinal detachments and corneal dysfunctions

Robert-Michael Kaplan, O.D., M.Ed.

NOTES

Other books from Beyond Words Publishing, Inc.

TIME WELL SPENT:
A Planner for Business and Health
by Larry Tobin, M.S.

A unique combination of a functional time management planner and an innovative year-long health program. It will help you take care of business while you take care of yourself! *Time Well Spent* is really three books in one: A concise 20-page orientation to stress management, a 52-week appointment planner, and a wellness guide to greater personal health.

$14.95, soft cover

WORKING WITH MEN
Professional Women Talk about Power, Sexuality, and Ethics
by Beth Milwid, Ph.D.

In the spirit of Studs Terkel's *WORKING,* psychologist Beth Milwid interviewed women across the country in a variety of industries and professions with the purpose of uncovering the truth about today's working women. These accounts provide insight and advice "from the trenches" and give an insider's look at the pressures that female colleagues, spouses and friends face very day. She discovered a new coalition developing inside corporate America ... based not on gender, race, or age, but rather on talent, mutual respect, and values.

$12.95, soft cover

MEN, WOMEN AND RELATIONSHIPS:
Making Peace with the Opposite Sex
by Dr. John Gray

In a balanced and respectful way, the strengths, needs, vulnerabilities, and mysteries unique to each sex are revealed. This understanding will help the reader lower tensions, release resentments and avoid misunderstandings with the opposite sex. Outlined are strategies for successfully giving and receiving emotional support, and creating more deeply satisfying and supportive relationships.

$12.95, soft cover